THE ACCOUNTING PRINCIPLES

The What, The Why, and the How

TABLE OF CONTENTS

Introduction

As a discipline, accounting is thousands of years old. Sure, back then, the IRS didn't exist - and the United States itself was not even an *idea*. But the very first seed of what we now call accounting is *ancient* (in the most literal sense of the word).

Accounting goes as far back as Mesopotamia. Needless to say, things then were very different - Mesopotamians did not even have the numbers we have today (which were introduced much later on), and neither did they have the same principles of accounting. We can take a fair bet that things were much simpler back then.

Ancient Egyptians and Babylonians continued the development of accounting by adding auditing systems to it as well. And by the time the Roman Empire came to rule the (known) world, their government already had the means to gain access to detailed financial information.

Somewhere towards the end of the 15th century, Luca Pacioli became the father of accounting and bookkeeping by becoming the first one to write a book on double-entry bookkeeping.

Even so, it took nearly four more centuries for the world to invent accounting as a profession, the way we see it today. It happened in Scotland. It was the 19th century already.

Today, accounting principles are used pretty much everywhere in the world. This book does not aim to portray the accounting principles of other states but hopes to debunk and clarify the main accounting principles used by accountants in the US.

We aim to go through the consecrated accounting principles, one by one, and explain what they are, and why they are important to follow. In addition to this, in the last chapter of our book, we also aim to walk you through the less popular accounting principles or, as they are frequently referred to, the *alternative* accounting principles.

Our main goal is to help you gain a better understanding of how accounting works - regardless of whether you are a business owner or a beginner at accounting.

Ten Important Terms

This chapter is dedicated to explaining some of the most important terms we will refer to throughout this book. Take this as a short glossary of terms. Keep in mind the meaning of the concepts described here and use it when learning about the basic accounting principles we will approach in this book.

1. Asset: Resources controlled by business entities are considered to be assets.

2. Liability: Obligations a company has at the present moment, which is the result of a past event. The result of this obligation is expected to lead to an outflow of assets from the entity.

3. Equity: Residual interest in the assets of a business entity once all the liabilities have been deduced.

4. Statement of comprehensive income: This is the report expressing the financial performance of a company. It is normally comprised from the income statement (which shows the profits and losses) and the statement of other comprehensive incomes.

5. Revenues: Boosts in economic benefit that come as an inflow of wealth, as an enhancement of an asset, or a decrease of liabilities that will boost the equity. It is important to note that contributions made by the owners, partners, or shareholders are not to be considered as revenue.

6. Expenses: Decreases in economic benefits that come as an outflow of wealth, depletion of an asset, or incurrence of liabilities that eventually lead to a drop in equity. The distributions made to the owners, partners, and shareholders of a company do not count as expenses.

7. Cash flow statement: Element of a financial statement, comprised out of the operating cash flow statement, investing cash flow statement, and financing cash flows.

8. Operating cash flow statement: The main activities that produce revenue in a company. When these are explained in a statement, the indirect method is used, meaning that profit and loss are adjusted for the effects of transactions that are non-cash in nature, past and future cash receipts or payments, and so on.

9. Investing cash flows: The acquisition of assets and other types of investments that are not normally included as cash equivalents.

10. Financing cash flows: Any activity that might alter the size of an equity or its composition, as well as the borrowings of the entity. Financing cash flows should always be included in financial statements because it will help potential investors and creditors predict the future cash flows of a company.

What are Accounting Principles?

The term "accounting principles" might sound odd - and downright scary - to someone who isn't involved in accounting in any way. However, things are much simpler when you look in-depth and understand that accounting principles have been adopted not because someone wanted to terrify young entrepreneurs and beginner accountants, but because they were *needed*.

In this chapter, we will go through the basic definition of accounting principles, how they came to be, why they are needed, and the two main groups of accounting principles: generally accepted accounting principles (or GAAP) and the alternative accounting principles (a set of accounting principles less common, but which might prove useful under specific circumstances as you read through this book).

Without further ado, let's dive in!

The Definition of Accounting Principles

The simplest way to define accounting principles is by calling them a "set of rules created to govern the entire field of accounting". In everyday terms, accounting principles are the very foundation upon which the more complex (and potentially more intriguing and interesting) regulations created around accounting are built.

Mind you, accounting principles have not always been the same - they were created along the way, as professionals in the field and regulators discovered the need for such rules to be implemented.

In the United States of America today, generally accepted accounting principles (GAAP) are strictly followed by everyone. Even more, if you want your company to be part of the stock exchange, you need to follow these basic rules to a T.

It is important to note that accounting principles are not the same all around the world and that sometimes, the difference between the regulations of one country and another might be staggering. In most developed markets, the principles stay more or less the same, with certain adjustments made to fit the economic and political landscape of those specific countries. In developing markets, however, things might be severely different - and this is why it is crucial that you hire the services of a local accounting expert if you want to expand your business to any other country on Earth.

The institution that deals with creating a uniform set of rules to govern accounting at a global level is called IASB (International Accounting Standards Board), but at the moment, there is no universally accepted set of accounting principles the entire (or at least the vast majority) world abides by.

Coming back home to the US, accounting principles here consist of three main pillars: the basic accounting principles and guidelines (the rules themselves), generally accepted industry practices (how the rules are and should be applied in "real life"), and the detailed rules issued by the FASB (Financial Accounting Standards Board) and by the Accounting Principles Board (APB).

As mentioned in the beginning, accounting principles have not been created and adopted to torment anyone trying to enter into this field of expertise, but rather with the purpose of *helping* them. In short, accounting principles help accountants and business owners achieve the following:

- Is useful to potential creditors, as well as potential investors, so that they have the full picture of what your business' books look like, both from an investment point of view and from that of the cash receipts and economic resources;

- As a resource to those who run the company to help them make sane financial decisions - short term and long-term alike;

- Is used by those who run the company to help them improve the way the business is performing;

- Useful in maintaining clean, clear, and coherent records of the company's financial state.

Generally Accepted Accounting Principles

If we look at accounting as a house, and consider accounting principles as its foundation, then the generally accepted accounting principles are pillars upon which the foundation is poured.

While not the only principles accountants abide by, GAAP are the principles everyone should follow - especially if the company is public and its financial records have to be available for potential investors, creditors, and shareholders.

Generally accepted accounting principles are based on the following goals:

1. The accountant has taken GAAP as the standard.

2. The same standards are to be applied throughout the entire reporting process so that any kind of errors and discrepancies are avoided.

3. If any standards are changed or updated, the accountant is expected to disclose and explain the reasoning behind the decision.

4. The accountant must be sincere in the depiction of the business' financial situation.

5. All the procedures used in financial reporting have to be consistent in time.

6. The accountant (and company) will not expect debt compensation despite showing both positives and negatives in their reports.

7. Speculation should be eliminated and financial data reporting should be fact-based.

8. All the report entries will be distributed across the right time periods (e.g. revenue is to be divided by its relevant time periods).

9. Full disclosure should be a goal of all financial reports.

10. When reporting, the assumption is that the business will continue to operate.

11. The parties involved in transactions should remain honest.

In order to achieve the aforementioned goals, generally accepted accounting principles have been split into twelve concepts: basic assumptions (four of them), basic principles (four of them) and basic constraints (five of them). They come as follows:

1. Basic assumptions: Business Entity, Going Concern, Monetary Unit, and Periodicity;

2. Basic Principles: Historical Cost, Revenue Recognition, Matching Principle, Full Disclosure Principle;

3. Basic Constraints: Objectivity, Materiality, Consistency, Conservatism, and Cost.

All of these generally accepted accounting principles will be dwelled upon in detail throughout this book, with each of them having a dedicated chapter for the explanations necessary in understanding their role and how they function.

The Alternative Accounting Principles

While we do not aim to go in-depth with these, it is important to be aware of their existence and of the fact that they are practiced as a complement to generally accepted accounting principles.

Most large companies simply abide by generally accepted accounting principles, as they are the most widely used and best understood rules in the financial community. However, in some cases, generally accepted accounting principles may be too broad or they simply may be incompatible with how some businesses function. For instance, a small business will find it difficult to follow the same guidelines as a large business, and additional accounting principles may be used.

These complementary or additional principles are sometimes referred to as *alternative* accounting principles - and we aim to explain some of them (as well as the *need* for them) throughout the last chapter of this book.

Why Are Accounting Principles Needed?

To someone working outside of the accounting and entrepreneurship field, accounting principles are but a set of regulations on paper.

To those who have already gained a little experience in accounting, these principles are the guidelines to doing *good work* - work that is consistent, work that is congruent, work that is relevant, and work that is honest both to internal stakeholders and to external investors and creditors.

The accounting principles are needed for one simple reason: there has to be a set of rules that govern how accounting is done across different industries, types of businesses and business purposes.

To help you understand the importance of accounting principles, think of them as the rules by which all drivers and pedestrians move around on the streets. Can you imagine a world without any kind of rules in place?

Probably not.

It would be complete chaos - and there are places in the world where traffic gets close to just that - complete anarchy. Picture this: everyone crosses the street wherever they want, however they want to, cars do not give each other priority when they should and they don't give pedestrians priority on crosswalks either.

Driving laws are more or less the same all around the world - with some exceptions, which are well-known and aggressively announced from the moment you step into those specific countries (e.g. the UK drives on the left side of the road, but this is a very well-known fact and it is announced on big banners everywhere, as soon as you enter the country regardless of the means by which you do that).

In accounting and financial reporting, there are no set international standards - but there *are* country-specific laws and regulations meant to make the reporting uniform and easily understandable by everyone.

Not having accounting principles in place means not having a basic understanding of how the traffic of financial reporting works. It means navigating aimlessly, on your own terms - but even worse, it could mean every business has the option of being unjust and dishonest with their reporting. How would investors know which business is worthy of their attention, then? How would stock markets themselves be able to assess the value of a share?

At this point, you may wonder and ask: *Yes, but generally accepted accounting principles haven't always been around.*

Indeed, they haven't. In fact, the group of standards and regulations we now call GAAP has been set for little over a decade. They *did* exist before that as well - but they consisted of exhaustive rules that allowed for plenty of error (intentional or not), and they constantly needed to be updated as soon as a new situation arose. Until 2002, when this problem was brought forward by multiple institutions (including the US Congress), accounting was ruled by fixed regulations, rather than *principles*.

The first accounting rules were set by the American Institute of Certified Public Accountants in 1939 through the Committee on Accounting Procedures, and they were subjected to the regulations of the US Securities and Exchange Commission. Later on, in 1959, the Committee on Accounting Procedures were replaced by the Accounting Principles Board, and in 1973, this became the Financial Accounting Standards Board. To date, they are the ones overseeing generally accepted accounting principles.

They were not always seen in a good light by both investors and the accounting community, though, not because their rules were too strict, but for the exact opposite. Until 2002, FASB oversaw a set of rules that were too ambiguous in terms of what should and shouldn't be done. This allowed accountants and audit professionals to find ways to circumvent them and to create new situations that were not stipulated in the set of rules the FASB enforced.

The entire situation generated a lot of turmoil in the financial world. In 2002, several famous cases brought the FASB system to the attention of the public and the US Congress. In the wake of several huge scandals (such as the one where Enron and the Arthur Andersen Firm were the main actors), equity holders in the US realized one very dangerous fact - they could not trust audit firms, and this needed to change.

We will not dive deeper into the Enron scandal, but the point we're trying to make is that it was one of the first moments that pushed for the creation of generally accepted accounting principles as they are known today. The loopholes and weaknesses of the previous system were aggressively exploited by Enron's auditors to mask the tremendous amount of debt the company was in. It was high time that this drove a change for a principle-based accounting standard.

And it did. While far from perfect (and still debated), generally accepted accounting principles are, thus far, a better and more comprehensive way of standardizing the industry's guidelines.

Generally accepted accounting principles are needed, and they *should* be followed. While some of them might be connected to actual US legislation, most of them are authoritative best practices (at their best). However, as the vast majority of companies abide by these rules (or, to be more precise, *principles*), it is important to do the same because it creates a sense of trustworthiness and coherence between businesses, creditors, and investors alike.

As mentioned before, some businesses don't take generally accepted accounting principles as they are. But we will dwell on this later on in the book when discussing alternative accounting principles.

As for the progress on delivering an international set of principles for accountants, it is still slow and steady - but with globalization becoming increasingly real and with trades being made across borders every day, this international set of principles is getting closer by the minute.

At the moment, the main hinge in the development of an internationally-accepted set of principles lies in, well, *methodology*. The International Financial Reporting Standards (IFRS) are more of a set of principles, whereas GAAP are a set of rules. The first ones make it easier for accountants to mold business reporting on the given set of principles but allow for misinterpretation and intentional mistakes. The latter ones, however, are strict and, at times, they make it difficult for businesses to mold financials to suit their needs.

As a note, this book is not meant to debate the efficiency of accounting principles, or their nature. It is an exhibition of what they are, why they are needed, and how they work in real life. Hopefully, the information presented below will help you understand why accounting works the way it does and why a set of principles to abide by is actually necessary in the context of businesses interacting with each other every day.

The Difference Between
Principles and Rules

Despite them being called *principles*, generally accepted accounting principles are very frequently seen as *rules* - but a clear distinction has to be made between the two terms if we are to continue with explanations on what each accounting principle is, why it exists, and how it should be followed.

To begin with, the Financial Accounting Standards Board (which we will continue to refer to as FASB) requires almost all companies to release financial statements according to specific standards. In the case of FASB (which is the authority for accounting standards in the United States of America), these standards function as *principles*, rather than rules.

The principles are used according to where the company is and the exact method they have chosen to follow when doing their accounting because, as you might know already, there are many ways to do this: cash accounting vs. accrual accounting, FIFO (First In, First Out) vs LIFO (Last In, First Out) , and so on.

There is an ongoing debate that's been sparked in the accounting world on whether rule-based or principle-based standards should be followed - and this debate is especially important in the light of scandals such as Enron (which we have touched upon in the previous chapter).

What is the main difference between the two, though? Well, it goes like this:

1. Principle-based accounting is, probably, the most popular method used around the world - and the reason most countries have adopted this is because it is frequently better to adjust accounting principle to the specificities of a company's transactions, rather than the other way around (adjusting the company transactions according to a given set of rules).

   The IFRS (International Financial Reporting Standards) system is principle-based as well. According to them, their system of standards should help to make financial statements more readable, easier to compare and understand, and more relevant to users.

   The main advantage of following a principle-based standardization system is connected to the fact that broader guidelines can very frequently be very practical. In the absence of a principle-based system, accountants might be forced to manipulate financial statements to fit into a very specific, given set of rules and this might create not only a lot of stress but further (legal) issues as well.

2. Rule-based accounting goes in the exact opposite direction of principle-based *accounting - meaning that it is comprised of a list of (very) detailed rules. These rules have to be followed in the creation of all financial statements that abide by rule-based accounting.*

   For accountants, the rule-based system is frequently easier to use because an absence of rules might have them facing court due to a bad judgment call on financial statements they have produced.

The generally accepted accounting principles, which we will discuss over the course of this book, are, in themselves, a rule-based system used in the USA. Similar systems exist in other parts of the world as well (such as the UK, for example).

Generally accepted accounting principles are to be followed by companies and their bookkeepers when financial statements are being produced. The main goal of generally accepted accounting principles is to provide investors, creditors, and other financial statement users with a way to compare the information provided by different companies (or by the same company when its financial statements are compared year by year).

The main advantage of the GAAP system (or any other rule-based system) is that the potentiality of a lawsuit occurring as a result of a released financial statement is lower than in the case of the principle-based systems. Accuracy can be increased and potential errors and ambiguity can be reduced by the use of the GAAP system.

The Issues with Both the Rule-Based and the Principle-Based Systems

Each of the aforementioned systems functions in its own way, providing specific advantages. However, both of them have flaws as well, and the main issue with both of the approaches is connected to the fact that there is no universally adopted accounting method.

When doing business solely in the US, this is not a problem. However, with 110 countries abiding by the IFRS (principle-based) accounting standards and the US being one of the few that uses the GAAP (rule-based) standard, this might be a problem if you want to do business outside of the borders of the United States of America.

When investments, mergers, or acquisitions take place involving parties that use different accounting systems, a different lens has to be used. For instance, Exxon and BP use different accounting methods, so halfway solutions would have to be found.

On the one hand, critics of the principle-based system(s) claim that this kind of method gives businesses too much leeway and they are not obliged to be transparent. In this point of view, a rule-based system would make the reports much more accurate when it comes to the financial health of a business.

On the other hand, rule-based methods have their flaws as well - precisely because complex rules can create a lot of complications. This system pushes bookkeepers to make businesses more profitable on paper, precisely because there is a huge responsibility to the shareholders of that business. Enron falls in this category, proving that a rule-based system can lead to many issues as well.

As a conclusion to this incursion into the differences between rule-based and principle-based methods, one element remains intact - the information provided in a company's financial statements has to be relevant and reliable at all times. Even more, it needs to be easy to compare (both from one accounting period to another and from one business entity to another as well).

We might see the end of rule-based accounting in the United States of America - but there is still a long and winding road to walk, as most specialists agree that while the principle-based system might be better from certain points of view, it also needs some serious alterations to prove efficient.

Until then, though, GAAP remains the foundation of American accounting. With its positives and its negatives, the generally accepted accounting principles system is the most common bookkeeping standard in the US and it will continue to be so - at least for the time being.

Following this, we will dive deeper into the core GAAP rules and what they mean, what their "ruling" status is, and how to incorporate them in your accounting.

Once done with that, we will proceed with alternatives to the GAAP system as well - not because they have to be used at all times, but because we do need to prove that generally accepted accounting principles are not to *always* be used (and that, yes, not using them, can have further implications as well).

Please keep in mind that this book aims to simplify these terms and explain them in an easy way. Look at this resource as a helper in the art of accounting at a beginner level, rather than an authoritative and very detailed explanation of why certain rules exist and how they can be followed.

GAAP is not about legislation per se - but it is tightly-knit into actual legislation. In general, following generally accepted accounting principles is meant to help you follow legislation and avoid further issues that would derive from not doing so. There are, however, exceptions to the rules - because even laws themselves frequently allow for little escapades (which frequently generate not-so-little scandals).

Whenever you can, however, you should adhere to the GAAP rules. They are there to help you navigate the intricate paths of American legislation in the financial sector, helping you, as an accountant, owner, or manager, better handle the financial statements you release to the public and avoid serious implications on a legal level.

The Business
Entity Principle

It is extremely easy to be confused when encountering a term like this - but in practice, the business entity principle is much easier to understand and it makes perfect sense once you understand the underlying assumption behind it.

Before jumping into the actual Business Entity Assumption, you must first understand the main difference between the different types of business proprietorship:

1. Sole proprietorship. This is the simplest form of business from the point of view of the proprietorship. Basically, it refers to businesses where only one individual is the owner of the company. For instance, if you open a local bakery shop on your own, you are the sole proprietor of this business. Keep in mind that this means that you are personally liable for the debts of your company too!

2. Partnership. This form of business association involves two or more individuals becoming the owners of a business. For instance, if you and a friend open a local bakery shop together, you are partners in this business.

3. Corporation. This is the most complex form of business from a proprietorship standpoint. It is also a very popular form of business because it protects the owners with limited personal liability, unlike in the case of a sole proprietorship.

The business entity principle (or assumption) is sometimes referred to as the economic entity principle (or assumption) and is based on the idea that the business owner(s) and the business might be legally associated and considered as one entity (such as in the case of a sole proprietorship business), but they should be considered as separate entities from an accounting point of view.

Therefore, the transactions of a business should always be recorded separately from those of its owner(s). This means the accountant has to use different accounting organizations - one for the organization (which will 100% exclude any kind of assets and/or liabilities the owner or any other entity might hold), and one for the owner (in case the owner has hired an accountant for the better management of their personal finances).

This assumption (principle) is needed because without its existence, it is very easy for the records of more than one entity to be intermingled. This would make it extremely difficult to understand what profits go where, and who should be taxed for what.

Examples of How the Business Entity Principle Is Applied

Let's look at an example to give you a better understanding of why the business entity principle must be followed:

- Let's say that you own a sock company and that you are the sole proprietor of this business. As the sole shareholder, your business issues to you a distribution of $200. In the company books, this means a reduction of equity worth $200 should be logged. In your personal books as the shareholder, this means you should add a total of $200 of taxable income.

- Let's go even deeper. Let's say that you own a tarot reading business and that your company acquires a house to run the operations from a more intimate space. The house is not the property of the company you run, but it is your property, as an individual. So, to make sure everything is legal, you will basically rent your house to your company for the modest price of $1,000/ month. For your company, this becomes a valid expense (so your accountant can use it in your bookkeeping). For you as an individual, the $1,000 you receive from your own business, this is taxable income.

- Let's take a third example. Let's say you run a software company that has just started out and needs money to move forward. As an individual and as the business owner, you loan your company $10,000 to keep it running smoothly. In the financial records, your accountant needs to show this as a liability. In your personal books, this should be a loan receivable.

The business entity principle allows for each business entity to be taxed separately. It also is a very much needed concept to help calculate the financial performance and/or position of a business entity.

Furthermore, the business entity principle is extremely useful when an organization is liquidated, as it will help determine the payout for each of the owners (in case there are multiple).

In the event of a lawsuit against a business, the business entity principle is needed because it will help with the ascertainment of the available assets from a liability point of view.

Last, but definitely not least, the business entity principle is needed when running an audit of the business records, when those records have been combined with those of other entities and/or individuals.

According to the business entity principle, all the financial transactions made by a business should be assigned to a specific business entity (e.g. "My Company LLC"). You and your business cannot mix your accounting records, assets, or bank accounts. In other words, you cannot pay for suppliers with your own credit card, but instead, use the money in your company's bank account. If your company is short on cash, you can either *loan* money to your own business, or you can sell its shares to yourself.

Are There Any Exemptions in the Business Entity Principle?
The only financial entity that is exempted from the Economic Entity Principle are subsidiaries and their parent companies. In these cases, financial statements of businesses can be combined into one, but even so, a special process called group consolidation is needed.

The Business Entity Assumption might be a little more difficult to grasp with small businesses and sole traders or freelancers - especially when they are just starting out and they might (inadvertently) combine their personal finances and the finances of their businesses.

For instance, when you are setting up a business, you will most likely need an initial investment. Some entrepreneurs are lucky enough to secure the capital from a business angel or a crowdfunding campaign.

If, however, this is not your case, you will have to record your initial investment as a capital investment (and do this officially, in business records). Likewise, if you buy computers for your company using your personal credit card, this should also be recorded as a capital investment.

The Business Entity Principle and the Limited Liability Concept

Another issue that must be tackled under this chapter is that of the difference between the economic entity principle and that of the limited liability. While the first is a principle accountant should abide by, the latter is an actual legal distinction between a business, the owner of that business, and the potential stakeholders of that business.

On the surface, there might not be many differences between the two, aside from the fact that one is an accounting guideline and the other is a legal regulation. In-depth, however, there is one more very important distinction to be made: the economic entity assumption is valid for all business forms, no matter what their structure may be. However, limited liability will not be applied to specific business structures, such as sole traders, for example.

What Happens If You Don't Respect the Business Entity Principle?

As explained before, most of the general accounting principles are guidelines for how financial reporting should be done correctly. And although not all of these principles might be directly tied into legislation (like in the case of the business entity assumption and the legal concept of limited liability), most of them will have serious legal implications in case something goes wrong (e.g. an investor puts money into a business that has falsely reported their financial status and discovers this later on can sue the liable parts for this).

Not respecting the business entity principle has very direct legal implications, precisely because it is almost synonymous with the concept of limited liability (in most cases, at least).

Transferring money from your account into that of your business and the other way around without recording it the proper way in your books will eventually lead to major issues from taxation, liquidation, or other similar events' point of view. This is why the business entity principle exists and why you should follow it!

The Monetary Unit Principle

The monetary unit principle (also known as the monetary unit assumption) is, like the business entity principle, a term that might feel odd or confusing to those who work outside of the accounting field. However, it can also be explained in very simple terms.

In short, the monetary unit principle says that you can only record business transactions expressed in a currency. For instance, you would not be able to record unquantifiable items (e.g. customer service quality of staff).

Furthermore, the monetary unit principle also implies that the value of the currency unity you are recording transactions into remains more or less stable in time.

The main goal of the monetary unit principle is that of making sure that everything recorded in financial statements is measurable in one way or another. The second main goal, is that all of these financial statements are measurable by a stable and reliable currency.

Which brings us to...

The Issue with the Monetary Unit Principle

Overall, the monetary unit principle is a very fair assumption - because, in the end, you do want all of your business transactions to be recorded in units that have value. And money does.

The main issue with this principle starts with the second part of the assumption - that the currency in which the value is expressed remains stable over time. In the US, FASB does not recognize the fact that inflation and currency devaluation can have an impact on financial reports. And it makes perfect sense to do that, given that American inflation has been quite stable over the past several years.

However, if you look deeper, even here, in the US, the value attributed to money has changed drastically over time. For instance, if your parents bought a house with $50,000 in the 1950s, their house might be valued at $1,000,000 now. This does not affect individuals as much in terms of how they do their taxes - but it might affect the value of a company. If, for instance, that house were a factory for your business, the financial reports on it would be inconsistent and they might even come across as dishonest because the house would not be valued for the same amount of money today.

In the US, it seems that this loophole in the monetary unit principle is not causing damage. In a hyperinflationary economy, however - such as Brazil, for example - this might be an issue and a company might have to restate their financial statements on a regular basis, precisely because the rapid devaluation of a currency can cause severe inadvertencies in how the reports are understood and interpreted (both internally and externally, when the business is analyzed by a potential investor or creditor, for example).

If the US economy were to become hyperinflationary, FASB would have to recognize the effects inflation can have when it comes to financial reporting. However, since this is highly unlikely in the current economic landscape, they probably won't do this.

The Second (Non)Issue with the Monetary Unit Principle

The second issue with the monetary unit principle is that it only considers currency as a valid measurable unit.

That makes perfect sense because you cannot measure the talent of your engineering team or the dedication of your entire customer service team.

However, some may argue that although they may not be quantifiable, a smart engineering team, an amiable customer service team, or simply a company that consists of people who are genuinely passionate can move mountains - and financial statements might not be able to help investors predict this, precisely because they are limited by the monetary unit principle.

On the other hand, nothing stops investors from going beyond financial statements to dig deeper into human resources, company morale, and company culture to ascertain whether or not they are worthy of investing in. Even more, how does one actually assess how intelligent, dedicated, or talented a company is, if there is no way to do this? Trusting the owners might not be a good idea, and since these are *human* resources, it is unlikely that they are 100% consistent over time (or that they will spend the next few years working for the same company).

From a business standpoint, yes, the monetary unit principle might be limiting but from an accounting and financial standpoint, it makes all the sense in the world. Can you imagine how people would measure the talent, dedication, or willingness to work extra hours in a company? It is thoroughly impossible, and not because of the monetary principle in itself, but simply because those skills, although valid and extremely valuable, cannot be measured.

The Periodicity Principle

The periodicity assumption is very simple to understand: any organization can report their financial results within a specified, designated period of time. In other words, entities have to send in consistent reports on their results and their cash flow monthly, quarterly, or annually.

Because reporting needs to be easy to compare and contrast, these time periods have to be kept the same over time. For instance, if you have to send your financial reports on the 5th of every month in 2019, you have to do the same in 2020, 2025, and 2070 as well.

There are some situations when consistency cannot be followed in terms of accounting periods. The two main cases when this happens include the following:

1. The entity started or ended their operations on an odd date and that one period is abbreviated. For instance, if all reporting must be done on the 5th of every month, but your business had started its operations on the 21st, you will report your first month of business from the 21st onwards, following that you will report it on the 5th of the second month of operations.

2. The entity does its reports on a four-week period. When this happens, there will be 13 reporting periods in a year - and while

this might not pose any issues internally, it might be incompatible with income statements when they are compared to those of an entity that uses a monthly report. For instance, if your business does four-week reports, and is compared with a competitor who does monthly reports, there might be inconsistencies when the reports are compared.

The Main Issue with the Periodicity Principle

One of the main problems debated in the accounting world about the periodicity principle is whether it is best to produce quarterly financial statements or monthly ones. In most cases, companies come out with monthly statements - not because it is compulsory, but because it allows them to closely monitor the efficiency of their business.

It is, however, more than worth mentioning that the Securities and Exchange Commission requires publicly-held companies to release quarterly statements. In most cases, they will release these, as well as additional monthly statements to be used internally, so that they can track the efficiency of the methods they have implemented to grow their business.

It is also very important to note that once the standard periods are set up, the accounting procedures of a company should be designed to provide ongoing, standardized production of financial statements for the periods they have designated. Consequently, a schedule of activities will announce when accruals are meant to be posted and how the standard structure of the journal entries should look.

The periodicity principle might sometimes come in partial contradiction with another accounting principle we will discuss further on in this book (the going concern assumption). As you will see later on, this principle says that businesses should be treated based on the idea that they will continue for an indefinite period of time.

However, periodic business performance assessments provide a shorter time frame, and they come (partially) in contradiction with the idea that a business will continue for an indefinite amount of time.

These are, however, very theoretical issues. In practice, both the going concern assumption and the periodicity principle are closely followed - one of them helps accountants provide statements that are focused on the long-term survival of a business, while the other one is helpful for investors and creditors who might want to closely monitor the performance of a business.

For example, one investor might look at quarterly financial statements to make a prediction related to what the business performance will be throughout the following quarter. Without the periodicity assumption, they wouldn't have access to this type of information - and thus, they would go in blindly, not knowing exactly what the business performance has been since the last major report.

Accounting Relevance vs. Reliability

To help you gain a deeper understanding of how the periodicity assumption is used, we will take some examples and relay them to you.

In general, this accounting principle is seen as a compromise solution between accounting relevance and relativity. Accounting relevance would normally be provided when longer-term statements are released. However, outside users of the financial statements will most likely want to get their hands on financial information as soon as possible, so that they can take a relevant decision (on whether or not they should invest or credit the company).

It is important to note that the more frequently the information is issued, the less reliable it is. For example, when a company releases monthly financial statements, investors can see great performance-related info in a relatively short amount of time. However, these monthly financial statements tend to be a lot less reliable, precisely because they do not paint a big, accurate picture of where the business stands from a financial point of view.

As a very concrete example: if you own a toy store and release your monthly statement in December, your investors will see a huge growth in numbers. However, that growth is not stable, but it is fueled by December being a month when people tend to spend more on toys (for their children's presents).

Adjacent Concepts to the Periodicity Assumption

To understand the periodicity principle even better, you might want to dive deeper into two other concepts: the matching concept and the revenue recognition principle (both which will be discussed at large later on in this book as well).

Both of these concepts dictate when businesses should allocate expenses and record revenue in terms of time periods. For example, if you are a sole trader and bill your clients on the 31st, but only get paid on the 5th of the following month, you will have to record the bill on the 31st as revenue for the current month.

Last, but definitely not least, if you want to see a very clear example of how the periodicity assumption works. The income statement is where you should look. This statement will present snippets of the business performance for a specific time period (e.g. a year-end income statement will show the income, as well as the expenses recorded by a company in a year).

It is quite important not to mistake income statements with balance sheets. While the first are issued for a more extended period of time, the second show what happened to a company (from a financial point of view) on a single date. The income statement reflects a period of time (month, quarter, year), while the balance sheet reflects a moment (one day in a month, for example).

Understanding The Financial Calendar

One of the best ways to understand why the financial calendar (fiscal year) works the way it does is by looking at it through the prism of the periodicity principle.

An accounting period will most often consist of 12 months. Still, depending on your jurisdiction, the beginning of these 12 months might differ. While one jurisdiction will start the fiscal year in January and end it in December, another one might start it in April and end it in March.

The International Financial Reporting Standards also mention that an accounting period does not consist of 365 days (a regular calendar year), but 52 weeks. In the UK and the British Commonwealth, this is referred to as the "4-4-5 calendar" and the US, it is referred to as the "52-53 week fiscal year".

In some cases, the financial year might consist of more than 12 accounting periods. In these situations, the "Year Open" period is counted from the moment the carried over balances (from the previous fiscal year are cleared), and the "Year Close" is considered when all the transactions are closed during one financial year.

The 52-53-week fiscal year/ 4-4-5 calendar is the best option to use when you want your company's fiscal year to always end on the same day of the week. There's no rule as to which day of the week this should be - Saturday and Sunday are most common because a lot of businesses are closed for inventory on these days, so it makes sense that the fiscal year ends then too.

There are two main ways to make sure this happens:

1. End the fiscal year on the last Saturday of the month when the fiscal year should end. For instance, if your fiscal year end month is in November, your business' year-end will most likely fall on any of the dates between November 25 and November 31.

   From the point of view of the actual calendar, this means that your company's year-end will move one day earlier every year (and two days earlier in leap years). After a few years, it will reach the point where the fiscal year end will be one full week before the end of the month (so if, when you started, your year-end was on November 31st, after a while, it would become November 25). This will reset the end of the fiscal year back to the end of the month (November 31st), and the fiscal year will be 53 weeks instead of the normal 52.

2. Place the Saturday that is nearest to the end of the month as the end of the company's fiscal year. For instance, if the fiscal year end month is March, you could end the fiscal year on the last Saturday of the month.

Similar to the previous example, the end of the fiscal year will move one day earlier every year (with the exception of leap years, when it will move two days earlier). When you reach the year when your fiscal year ends four days before the end of the month, the date will move to the Saturday of the next month, and thus, the entire calculus will be reset. That fiscal year will have 53 weeks, instead of 52.

The mathematics behind the periodicity principle can get complicated at times - but it is of the utmost importance that you stick to it. Like most of the generally accepted accounting principles, the periodicity assumption is tightly connected with all of the other principles and rules - so if you have to follow GAAP, you will have to follow this principle as well. For instance, if you want to follow the consistency constraint, you will automatically have to assume the periodicity principle as well, since the time at which you make your financial reports available should be consistent from one accounting period to the next one.

The Going Concern Principle

This principle was mentioned in the previous chapter and, at its very foundation, is very easy to understand.

This accounting principle is based on the assumption that a business will continue to exist - in the near, medium, and potentially far future as well. Or, put in even simpler words, a business will not liquidate (or it will not be forced out of business in any way).

The going concern assumption is considered a basic accounting principle because it serves as a guideline that allows potential investors and creditors to assume that the business will be fully operational to carry on with its objectives, obligations, and commitments. Or, even simpler: a business is a going concern if they do not plan on selling everything in the future. They are not a going concern if they plan on selling or liquidating in the future.

For a short clarification of terms, we will mention here that "future" refers to anything foreseeable. You may not know where your business will be in 10 years from now but you do know that you want to continue operations for the following year (and the numbers show that you have the capacity to do so).

Why Is It Important?

The going concern assumption is a very important element of generally accepted accounting principles. Without it, no business would ever be able to perform any kind of prepaid expenses because no business would ever be able to defer their prepaid expenses to future accounting periods.

To understand the importance of this accounting principle, assume that a business will not be able to carry out their obligations, objectives, and commitments in the foreseeable future. If you would know this about a business, you would not allow it to prepay (or accrue) any kind of service or good.

The Going Concern vs. the Cost Principle

The going concern principle is not only tightly connected to the periodicity principle, as shown in the previous chapter, but it is also connected to the cost principle and it actually provides bookkeepers with justification to follow it.

Put it this way: if your business is a going concern, you have no intention of liquidating it. Therefore, you do not have to report the current value of your assets (the long term ones). If, for example, an asset has been damaged, its carrying amount would be reduced to an amount that is actually lower (sometimes by a lot) than its carrying value.

The going concern principle is used when calculating the depreciation of assets. Basically, this calculation is based on the expected economic life an asset is estimated to have, and not on its actual market value. It is because of this specific accounting principle that assets are always reported on the balance sheet using their historical cost, rather than an updated one (that takes inflation into consideration).

According to the going concern principle, a company will automatically assume that its operations will continue for an indefinite time in the future. Therefore, their assets will be used until they are fully depreciated.

If the going concern principle isn't taken into consideration, it means that the business has the potential to close within the next twelve months. Therefore, it would be more appropriate to adopt a liquidation approach.

So, what happens if a business *does* pose a serious risk of closing in the foreseeable future?

If a business' financial statements point in a bankruptcy direction, then the going concern assumption shouldn't be followed. In this case, the statements should have some sort of disclosure that discusses the going concern and the current status of the company.

The going concern principle is a basic assumption - there's no point in analyzing a company's statements (as an investor or as a creditor alike) if there's a suspicion that the company will not continue its operations. Sure, in the event you want to sell a business that's not a going concern, and you are solely selling it for its assets, then yes, potential buyers will surely want to read the financial report. Aside from that though, the going concern principle is one of the most logical accounting principles!

How is the Going Concern Principle Used?

The going concern principle has been debated and shown in the media by a lot of companies.

For instance, take General Motors. Nearly two decades ago, GM was expecting to go through severe financial difficulties. In fact, they were in so much trouble that they almost declared bankruptcy and closed all of their operations all over the world.

In their case, the Federal Government helped by giving them a bailout and a guarantee. If it weren't for the government, General Motors wouldn't have continued to be considered a going concern (as they were on the brink of collapse). However, because the Federal government helped them, there was no reason to believe that the company would cease to operate in the foreseeable future.

Is there any chance GM will stop their operations in the future?

Probably, yes.

But that doesn't mean that GM isn't at the moment a going concern. If they found themselves in the same situation as they did in the early 2000s, they would not be a going concern (provided that the government didn't step in for them again).

Let's take another example: if you own a very small software company that only works on one software application and an IT giant is suing you for copyright infringement, this lawsuit could mean the end of your business. If there's a chance that this large IT company could win the lawsuit (which is usually the case), then this means that your business would not be a going concern. In other words, your business is at risk, so it cannot be safely assumed that it will continue its operations one year from now.

The Historical
Cost Principle

The historical cost principle is, by far, one of the more confusing generally accepted accounting principles - and mostly because it is frequently poorly explained and poorly understood.

We do aim, however, to paint an accurate picture of what this accounting principle is - especially as it is one of the single most important ones.

To begin with, keep in mind that the historical cost principle is not an assumption (like the ones we have been describing thus far), but an actual principle. This means that it will most likely be a little more intricate - but don't let this scare you off. Once you have it clearly set in your mind, it will never go away!

Basically, the historical cost principle refers to the original cost of an asset.

Simple, right?

This accounting principle has become a key element for all bookkeepers because the historical cost is almost always used in financial statements and balance sheets (when referring to assets, at least). It is, in many ways, a *de facto* in the bookkeeping world, and it makes a lot of sense for it to be so, once you understand the underlying motivation behind it.

It is worth noting that not *all* assets are actually held at historical cost. For instance, any kind of marketable security will be held at market value on every balance sheet created by the company's accountants.

Also, keep in mind that not only assets are accounted for based on the historical cost principle, but liabilities are accounted for in the same way as well. Any kind of bond or debt will be logged on the balance sheet at its initial price of acquisition.

Important Terms

Before diving deeper into the concept of historical cost, it is worth making a clear distinction between the historical cost (i.e. the original cost of an asset) and other types of costs that might appear on company books:

1. Replacement costs. This is the amount of money an asset purchased in the past would be valued at today. Sometimes, accountants refer to this cost as a "current cost".

2. Inflation-adjusted costs. As the name suggests, this term is used to describe the increased value of an asset, which reflects a rise in inflation (as compared to the original time of purchase).

3. Market value. This is the potential amount a company's asset could be sold for, based on how many buyers there are and what the market's desire to buy that asset is. Or, in other words, this is a value assigned to an asset-based on how much buyers would (at least theoretically) be willing to pay for it.

The Main Concern with the Historical Cost Principle

Probably the most confusing aspect of the historical cost principle (and the most debated one) is connected to asset depreciation.

The reason that assets are valued at their historical cost (as opposed to the current market value) is because it prevents accountants from overestimating an asset's value when this appreciation may be the result of nothing more than volatile market conditions.

Even more, the use of the historical cost principle is tightly connected to the conservatism concern (another accounting principle we will dwell upon a bit later on in the book). Basically, this principle states that any asset depreciation must be both noted and compared to that asset's historical cost. This is normally used for long-term assets (such as buildings or larger pieces of machinery that help the business in its operations).

When it comes to the balance sheet, the annual depreciation of assets should be accumulated over the passing of years, and then it should be recorded right below that asset's historical cost. To ensure that the asset will not be overstated in terms of value, the total depreciation is subtracted from the historical cost (which results in a lower net asset value).

Asset impairment is another concern connected to the historical cost principle. This is not connected to actual depreciation (which usually includes the actual physical wear and tear of assets over a longer period of time). Asset impairment, however, can occur at any time when it comes to specific assets, even if they are not physical (e.g. goodwill).

When asset impairment happens, that asset's market value drops below what it was originally worth and what it was originally listed as on the company's balance sheet. To bring it back, companies use an asset impairment charge (which is considered to be a restructuring cost) when reevaluating the value of those given assets, and make business changes.

In these circumstances, it is best if the devaluation of the asset is based on the current conditions of the market, as opposed to calculating everything according to its historical cost.

It is worth noting that when an asset depreciates as a result of asset impairment, this loss will directly impact the company's profits.

There are cases when the historical cost principle is not applied. Instead, a practice known as "market-to-market" is used. Using this method, the balance sheet will be updated accordingly when a market moves (and the numbers can go either up or down, depending on how the market itself moves).

Normally, this practice is applied when talking about assets that are held for sale, because those assets' market value can be used in making predictions of future cash flow that might result from potential sales.

For instance, marketable securities fall in this category when they are held for trading purposes. In these cases, the market might swing (and by a lot), and these securities will be marked accordingly: upward or downward, reflecting their true value under the specificities of market conditions.

The Compromise Solution

As in the case of the periodicity principle, the historical cost is a compromise solution between two goals accountants have: to be reliable and to provide useful information.

Using the historical cost of an asset will make you reliable. It is as clear as day - that is the price you paid for an asset when it was purchased - and whether it was ten, twenty, or one hundred years ago does not make the statement falser in any way.

At the same time, the historical cost is not extremely useful. To the outside watcher, it doesn't say much if a company bought a house for $20,000 in the 1950s because, without adjusting the price to inflation and the current market, that number doesn't say much to investors and/or creditors about the asset's worth.

In this case, using a fair market value price (as described earlier on in this chapter) would most likely be more useful. There is a major issue with this, though: the fair market value price leaves a lot to opinions (which could be based on false estimates and make the statements completely unreliable). Therefore, FASB has decided that the historical cost principle is the better option and that it should be used in the vast majority of situations. This might change in the future, as both FASB and IASB have become a bit more open to the concept of fair value and they might find a way to adopt it too.

To help you understand the historical cost principle and how it is used, here are two clear examples:

Let's say your grandfather founded a restaurant in the 1940s and that it was based in a building your grandfather had purchased for $20,000. You now own the restaurant, as it has been passed down from one generation to another. Your balance sheet will show the building's price was $20,000, but taking inflation and the current market value into consideration, that building is now worth $200,000. However, until you sell the building or until it becomes impossible to use, the balance sheet will continue to show it as a $20,000 asset.

You are a seamstress and in 1999, you bought a professional sewing machine for $4000. After using it for 20 years, the machine is now worth less than $500. However, your reports will continue to show the machine as being worth $4,000, the original price you paid for it in 1999.

Of all accounting principles, the historical cost one can be the most confusing - but we promise it will make a lot more sense once you go through the entire book, precisely because all of these principles are intermingled and interdependent to some extent. The shortest explanation of why the historical cost principle is so important and so common is because it is the most reliable and non-opinion-based way of making sense of your expenses over time - and your reports have to be consistent, objective, and written in the spirit of full disclosure at all times.

The Revenue
Recognition Principle

The revenue recognition principle is used in accrual accounting (the type of accounting that records both expenses and revenue when they occur, not when the cash is actually received).

That is what the revenue recognition principle stands for: a business should record their revenue not when they receive the cash (or pay the cash), but when they are actually acknowledged.

Basically, the moment you send an invoice to a client, you already record it on your balance sheets. For instance, if you have provided marketing services to a client and they were worth $2,000, you will send the invoice at the end of February.

However, the client will not pay you for another three months, which means that the revenue will be *cashed in* only at the end of May - but it will be considered as "realized" at the end of January, when you delivered the services and sent the invoice. In accrual accounting, you will record the invoice on your balance sheets as if it already "happened" - and this is based on the revenue recognition principle.

In some ways, the revenue recognition principle is similar to the matching principle (which we will, of course, discuss later on in this book). The main similarity between the two is related to the fact that every activity should be recorded when it happens. The main difference, however, is that the revenue accounting principle only refers to revenue and the accounting period that they should be recorded in. At the same time, the matching principle talks about the expenses and the correct accounting period that they should be recorded in.

Both concepts are used in accrual accounting and lie at its very foundation. They are also basic generally accepted accounting principles, which makes them quite important especially for businesses who plan on going public, because it allows for a standardized method of bookkeeping that will not keep potential investors and creditors in the dark.

It is worth noting here that cash accounting is used as well. However, it tends to be less popular with businesses who want to go public, precisely because records might be unreliable (the cash might take some time to enter the flow, and thus, the records might be altered).

When is the Revenue Recognized?

There are some rules to guide accountants in knowing when to recognize the revenue (and thus, when to enter it in their books). In general, there are five steps that have to be followed for revenue to be considered as "recognized" and ready to be entered on the balance sheets:

1. There has to be some sort of link with a contractor. Most often, this is a written contract that has clearly defined their financial compensation. Sometimes, an oral arrangement can be used as well.

2. The performance obligations in the contract (written or verbal) have been noted. Put simply, a performance obligation is a point

the contractor has to meet as per the contract they have signed or agreed with. So, for instance, if you own a marketing company and you make 2,000 visits to your website a performance obligation, you have to deliver - and once that happens, you can take note of it.

3. The price of the transaction has to be determined. This means that, as a provider of services or goods, you have to determine the transaction price in your contract. This will become the amount of consideration your client has to pay in exchange for the services or goods you have delivered. Keep in mind that any kind of money collected on behalf of third parties (e.g. a copywriter your marketing firm has contracted for this specific project) should not be included in the transaction price.

4. The price of the transaction and the performance obligations should be matched through a process called "allocation process". Basically, you can allocate the price to the performance obligation that reflects the aforementioned amount of consideration you, as a seller, expect to receive when the performance obligation is satisfied. When determining this allocation, you have to first estimate the selling price of the services or goods you have delivered from the moment the contract started.

5. Recognize the revenue when the obligations are fulfilled (i.e. when the services or goods you are selling have been transferred to the customer). When the transfer is completed (the customer is in possession of the services or goods), the revenue can be recognized.

Exceptions from the Revenue Recognition Principle

While the revenue recognition principle is commonly used in accrual accounting, there are some exceptions as well. The main situations when the revenue recognition principle should not be used include the following:

1. In some cases, manufacturing businesses may have to recognize the revenue during the production process (as opposed to recognizing it when the products are sold). This is especially true in the case of long-term contractors (such as those working in defense or construction, for example). In these cases, the revenue will be realized (and then cashed in) at various stages in the process (e.g. when the foundation of a new building is laid, when the first floor is up, etc.).

2. In some cases, manufacturing companies will recognize the revenue once the process is done, but before the actual sale is done. For instance, this is commonly used in agriculture and mining - and the main reason this method is used in these industries is because the goods are good to go to market and sold as soon as they are mined, plucked, or harvested.

3. When accrual accounting is not used and when companies do their accounting on a cash basis, the revenue recognition principle is not followed (because, as explained before, it goes in contradiction with the type of accounting used). Companies that work based on installment sales are more commonly inclined to this accounting method.

Examples of How the Revenue Recognition Principle Is Used

To help you understand the concept of revenue recognition as a generally accepted accounting principle, here are two relevant examples:

1. You own an online clothing store that delivers its products to your customers' door. According to the revenue recognition principle, you will record the transaction in your balance sheets when the customer has possession of the products (e.g. the estimated time of delivery you have been given by the delivery company). It might take more than one week between that moment and the moment your products' worth will actually appear as cash for your company - but according to the basics of accrual accounting and the revenue recognition principle, this transaction should have been recorded in your balance sheets by then.

2. You are an accountant and you provide your client with $1,000 worth of services. You forward everything to them on the 1st of March, but they only pay the invoice next February, in 2020. There is a large time gap here, but your balance sheets will have recorded this transaction as of 1st of March, 2019.

The revenue recognition principle might not make sense 100% when you first stumble upon it. However, it is one of the fundamentals of accrual used for most businesses that focus on going public). As long as you can keep track of everything in a smart and steady way, the revenue recognition principle will help you stay consistent and track your financial numbers correctly.

The Matching Principle

As mentioned in the previous chapter, the matching principle is somewhat similar to the revenue recognition principle, but it focuses on a different side of financial transactions of a company.

To be more precise, the matching principle is a generally accepted accounting principle that says that expenses have to be recognized during the same reporting period that their related revenues have been recognized.

As also mentioned in the previous chapter, the matching principle is very tightly connected to accrual accounting (the accounting method where both revenue and expenses are recorded at the moment they are incurred, regardless of when the cash might be received) and to the revenue recognition principle (which we discussed earlier).

In cash accounting, neither the revenue recognition nor the matching principle is used, because in that case, all the transactions are recorded when cash is actually received from the client.

The Importance of the Matching Principle

In simple terms, the matching principle is important because it allows companies to adhere to a consistent method of measuring their financial statements (their balance sheets, their income statement, and so on).

If the expenses are not recognized at the right time, then the statements of a company might not be reliable at all, putting at risk the quality of their information and painting an inaccurate or downright false representation of the business' financial status.

For instance, if you recognize any kind of expense earlier than you should, this will show on your balance sheets as a lower income.

Likewise, if any kind of expense is recognized later than it should be, this will make the balance sheets appear as if they have a higher net income.

The reason the matching principle is used is because there are some business financial elements taking advantage of this principle. For instance, assets (long-term assets especially) will depreciate in time - but the use of the matching principle will allow accountants to spread out the matching appropriately, so that balance is achieved when it comes to incoming cash flow.

Furthermore, the matching principle will usually allow assets to be distributed and matched over the course of its economic life, until depreciation. This will help balance the cost over a given period of time.

Examples of How the Matching Principle Works

The matching principle makes bookkeepers register all the expenses in the moment they occur, not the moment the cash reaches the other side.

Some examples of how this works include the following:

1. You have hired a contracted salesman and you have to give them 5% commission on all the sales they have done in January (sales which have been recorded as revenue in January). The

commission itself will only be paid in February. However, the expense should be recorded in January, because that is when it occurred for the first time.

2. You own a small manufacturing company and you need a piece of machinery worth $10,000. The machinery will be used for 10 years, and then it will depreciate because that is its suggested useful life. When doing the bookkeeping, the cost of the equipment will have to be registered as a depreciation expense at $1,000 month for ten years.

3. You own a small fast food restaurant and you pay your employees on an hourly basis. Normally, the hourly period of payment will end on May 27, but your employees will actually continue to work until the end of the calendar month. Although you will pay the difference between May 27 and May 30 at the beginning of June, this will be on record for the month of May.

4. You have a retail store and you allow your customers to take extended lines of credit. This is a good move because statistically, people are more tempted to buy more if they have a credit card or line of credit (and this is precisely why almost all stores offer their own cards).

The extended terms help you generate more sales. However, this also means that all the costs associated with the extended terms should be recorded when the revenues are recorded as well (e.g. during the accounting period when the purchase was made, not the accounting period when the cash will reach your bank account.

One of the main issues that could arise from offering credit to customers is bad debt. Unfortunately, not all customers pay off their store debt - which would put you, as the store owner, in the position of having to collect the debt from your customers. This means that you would have to write off the receivable and add it in the bad debt category because it will never be collected (most likely).

The two main ways to deal with bad debts from an accounting point of view is to either write them off or to use the allowance method. Writing the debt off is not a good option because it doesn't match revenues and expenses (mostly because the bad debt will not be recorded unless the account becomes uncollectible and the revenues will have already been recorded).

To better match the revenues and the expenses, the allowance method is used. This means that when an account receivable is identified as uncollectible, the amount will be removed from the accounts receivable tab. This is only done on the balance sheet and no expense or loss will be added to the income statement (not because it is "hidden", but because this write-off will be covered by the previous adjusting entries for estimated bad debt expense).

In many ways, the matching principle is very similar to the revenue recognition principle - they are, in the end, facets of the same coin and they both state that whatever value comes into your company or goes out of it should be clearly stated in your financial reports. Both the matching principle and the revenue recognition one are there to help you, as an entrepreneur or accountant, to keep your numbers and your reporting consistent and clear from one accounting period to another.

The Full Disclosure Principle

The full disclosure principle is the last of the actual principles (following on, we will talk about constraints of generally accepted accounting principles). A quintessential part of every bookkeeper's work, the full disclosure principle is extremely important because it lies at the very foundation of honesty in the financial world.

Basically, the full disclosure principle requires companies to report all the necessary information about their business' financial statements (and all the other information that might be relevant). This information needs to be made available to anyone who is accustomed to readings of this kind.

Why Is the Full Disclosure Principle So Important?

The full disclosure principle is important for very obvious reasons: it helps investors and creditors make sure that the financial information they read in a company's financial statements is not misleading in any way (by omitting information, for example). For you as a company, this is important because it creates a sense of trust with your stakeholders - they will be aware, from the very beginning, that your statements are full and unequivocally true. This way, they will be able to make a better financial decision regarding your company.

The full disclosure principle forces managers and accountants to disclose *all* information that could be important and could affect the business and its financial situation. Manipulating your financial statements to make your company look stronger than it actually is is never a good idea as it can have serious legal implications in the event of a lawsuit. It also makes you far less trustworthy in everyone's eyes as well, virtually pushing you to the outskirts of the business world.

What Information Should Be Disclosed?

Everything should be shared on financial statements - from the transactions that have already occurred to financial events that will happen in the future and have been anticipated by your team (they can be revenue-based or expenses as well).

Transparency should be the keyword when it comes to financial statements, and they should always include any kind of information that might have an influence on the opinion an outsider makes on the company.

Any of the following types of information should be disclosed on financial statements:

- The accounting policies your company follows;

- Any kind of change you have made in the accounting systems, principles, as well as the justification for your changes;

- The financial statements themselves (including the footnotes and extra notes that provide clarification);

- Any kind of inventory losses you may have recorded (no matter what the reason behind this might be: obsoleteness, decrease, damage, and so on);

- Information on your non-monetary transactions and their nature;

- The description of any asset retirement obligations you may have;

- Whether you expect changes in VAT rates in the future;

- If a company sells one of their subsidiaries, the information should be there (even if the sale has been done behind closed doors, among the familiar faces of the company, such as between the company and the spouse of one of the executives);

- When transactions have large values, the nature of the relationship between the two parties (yours and that of the other business/entity) should be clearly described;

- Any kind of liabilities, contingencies, contingent assets, legal lawsuits/ proceedings, and so on.

Or, in simpler words, outside readers should be allowed to see everything about your company, regardless of the nature of those financial events. They need to have a bird's eye view on your business - and the full disclosure principle is there to ensure this.

It is also important to note that all of the financial statements released by your company should be easy to understand by everyone who lays eyes on them - no matter what their industry might be and what they might deal in.

In order for this to happen, it is extremely important to make sure you use footnotes correctly and that you clearly explain every single situation (including those that haven't happened just yet, but have a good chance of potentially happening in the near to medium future). Normally, lawsuits and contingencies are explained in the footnotes - but there's no rule against explaining other types of events, so *do* remember to use the footnotes to provide clarifications.

Supplemental information can be annexed to your financial statements as well. They are used when the information provided might be useful for investors and creditors, but might not be very reliable. For instance, if the management of a company wants to include their own analysis of the business growth, this could help investors a lot. However, since this would be an opinion-based piece, it shouldn't be considered as *fact*, so it should be added as supplemental information to your statements.

Examples of How the Full Disclosure Principle Works

To help you better understand how the full disclosure principle works and why it is so useful and important (especially to investors and creditors), read the following relevant examples:

1. Let's say you own a company that has just purchased a piece of land, which makes you the new owners of that property. A pedestrian passing by falls onto the piece of land and gets injured. They are now suing you for negligence, and the amount of money is not negligible at all - and given that this is very likely your fault, the pedestrian might actually win the lawsuit.

   According to the full disclosure principle, you are absolutely required to record this lawsuit and to make it public in your statements. This is, after all, an anticipated loss and it should be marked as a footnote in your financial statements - despite the loss not having been confirmed yet.

2. And here's another example: you are a national sock retailer and you have reported $50,000 in stock inventory last year. In the footnotes associated with the financial statements, your company should disclose the accounting policies used - such as the inventory valuation methods, for example (are they FIFO or LIFO?).

3. If your company has encumbered or pledged assets, the information should be released to the public using the financial statement footnotes. Going concerns, goodwill impairments, and other similar situations should definitely be disclosed on the financial statements and their footnotes as well.

All in all, the full disclosure principle is all about honesty and about clearly explaining the entries in your financial statements when further explanations are due. As mentioned before, not following this principle could attract serious consequences, including from a legal point of view - so, whenever in doubt, it's better to fully disclose the situation of your company and give your potential investors and creditors all the explanations they need to make it all clear. You don't want to leave room for interpretation, precisely because a lawsuit based on a false interpretation of numbers could have a severe impact on your company!

The Objectivity Principle

The objectivity principle is not a principle per se, but a constraint that is officially considered part of generally accepted accounting principles. As with the other GAAP rules, this one makes perfect sense once you grasp a better understanding of what it refers to and why it is so important.

Put simply, the objectivity principle says that all financial statements of a company should be based on solid evidence. The main purpose behind this accounting constraint is to keep all the management (and potentially the accountants dealing with a business) from producing financial statements that are based on opinions and biases, rather than actual facts.

The objectivity principle is comprised of two main parts: relevance and reliability. The concept of relevance means that financial statements should be accurate, and they should have a predictive and feedback-oriented value. Therefore, these financial statements can be used to predict the performance of a company in the future.

Reliability, on the other hand, means that all the financial information presented in a report can be verified from multiple points of view and sources. It also means that *all* the financial information is already presented, regardless of whether it is favorable or not.

Issues with the Objectivity Principle

This accounting principle goes beyond the idea that you shouldn't simply emit opinions of your business in financial statements. It also covers the potential assumptions you might make about future revenue and expenses as well - so, according to the objectivity principle, you shouldn't make assumptions about events you do not have enough information for (yet).

The objective point of view is necessary when creating financial statements, precisely because the result should provide information investors can actually rely on when making a thorough evaluation of the financial results and position, as well as the cash flow, of a business.

Furthermore, when external auditors are involved, they need their client companies to produce financial statements that are objective (and thus, created under the objectivity principle). In order to comply with this very important principle of generally accepted accounting principles, businesses should also make sure to have a very well-planned record archiving system in place. This will make it easier for any auditors to localize the information that will eventually support the aggregate balances entered in the company's financial statements.

Another important issue to note is that when an auditor has worked (internally) for a company, but now is assigned to do the audit of the same business, that specific auditor may not be 100% objective when it comes to the final audit report (and this depends on the former client and their relationship). Therefore, it is best if auditors assigned to manage the audit of a business have not had a different business relationship with the same company before.

Examples of How the Objectivity Principle Is Used

There are many instances when the objectivity principle in accounting should be considered. Here are some:

1. For instance, if you are the founder or CEO of a business, and you think that you will win a big lawsuit in the near future, you might be tempted to add this as revenue on your financial statements. However, according to the objectivity principle, you should first wait for more information on whether or not you will win the lawsuit, so that you do not make a false statement and make a false entry in your balance sheets and/or financial statements.

2. You are a manager in a company and you already own a large stake in it, your interest lies in reporting an optimistic result for the entire business. However, an objective point of view should be used in reporting. Therefore, you should allow someone else, an external auditor perhaps, to handle the reports of your company, so that external readers can have a full,

comprehensive, and objective view of where the company might be going in the near future from a financial point of view.

3. You are the accountant of a company and you are preparing financial statements for it. You ask for the company's financial records, to support the information related to its payables and receivables, but the company refuses to provide you with this info, claiming that it is too difficult to access it. The company suggests that you should simply use the numbers in the accounting system. However, this would go against the objectivity principle, since all financial statements have to be 100% based on verifiable and reliable records.

4. Your company purchased a plot of land three years ago, and its price was $20,000. You want to find out its value today, but asking five different experts in real estate will most likely lead to 5 different answers. While these answers might come from actual experts in the field, they are still opinions. So, the best way to record this in your financial statements is with the initial price you paid for it - $20,000, three years ago.

The Objectivity Principle and Intangible Assets

The objectivity principle extends to what should and shouldn't be included in your balance sheets. For instance, some very valuable assets will not appear on the balance sheet because, well, they are not measurable.

Let's say you have an impeccable reputation with all of your clients and they are all very loyal to you. Normally, these assets (or values, if you want to call them that) would increase your company's value. However, they are intangible in the sense that they cannot be measured - so they cannot be included in the financial statements of a company.

The only way to uphold the objectivity principle in these situations is when you add them in an appendix to your financial statement and the client who buys your business uses them in their own balance sheets (usually marking them as "goodwill"), so that an explanation is provided as to why they paid more for your business when they purchased it.

As you can see, the objectivity principle touches upon everything connected to accounting and lies at the very foundation of what professional bookkeeping should be. As in the case of the other principles presented in this book, it can be said that not respecting this principle could attract serious issues - even issues of a legal nature. Depending on your mistake, this could be connected to actual legislation, or it simply could generate a lawsuit that would eventually have a negative impact on your business (or the business you work for, for that matter).

The Materiality Principle

The materiality principle, also known as the materiality concept or the materiality constraint is another very important generally accepted accounting principle to consider (as are all the principles we have discussed and will continue to discuss, for that matter).

The materiality concern expresses that a company can forego another accounting principle *only* if the amount discussed is small (in the sense that it is small enough not to mislead financial statement readers in any way).

Except in these kinds of situations, bookkeepers should follow generally accepted accounting principles and practices at all times. If ignoring the rules will make no difference whatsoever, or if following the rules would be much too expensive for the company, the accountants are allowed to ignore the accounting principles.

The main idea behind the materiality principle is that some transactions or amounts can actually be ignored because they will not affect the grand scheme of the company and they do not have to be treated in the same manner as other, bigger transactions (also known as material transactions).

How to Define What Is Material and What Is Immaterial?

You might be tempted to think that the materiality principle will basically annihilate all of the other accounting principles, because accountants and management can always argue that a transaction was not meant to affect the grand scheme of things (and thus, it could be ignored in financial statements).

However, it is very important to note that knowing the difference between what can be considered material or immaterial is to be quite clearly understood by the accountant. It is crucial, thus, that the accountant has a very clear judgment and that they proceed according to the full disclosure principle at all times (which implies that they will also know the difference between material and immaterial).

Most of the times, this is a judgment call. For the local bakery, $5,000 may be a very big sum of money and they will not be able to consider it as immaterial. However, for a very large multinational corporation (e.g. Microsoft), this might not mean much - and thus, they can consider it immaterial as long as it does not affect the way potential investors and creditors read the financial statements of the company.

Materiality (or immateriality, for that matter) cannot be defined in terms of monetary value alone. It is, in the end, a matter of the *nature* of the item that is being questioned as well. Therefore, aside from the monetary amount per se, the bookkeeper will also have to consider whether or not the item will involve an unlawful transaction, as well as other factors that might determine its materiality.

Materiality is a concept relative in both size and importance. Most of the times, the judgment call is obvious, especially if you have a broader understanding of a business' financial status (which you should if you are their accountant or part of their accounting team). Of course, every situation and every company is different but when in doubt, however, you have to narrow it down to one question: will you paint a misleading picture of the company's financial status if you omit any generally accepted accounting principles?

Examples of How the Materiality Principle Is Used

To help you understand the materiality principle, here are some focused examples:

1. If you are a company controller, you decide that the materiality constraint is $10.000. If any asset is purchased by the company below that sum of money, the size of the purchase can be considered below the materiality level - and thus, the accountant will add this purchase as an expense, rather than a fixed asset (which might depreciate over the years).

   If, however, the same company wants to include a $15,000 insurance policy as an expense, as opposed to an asset, this cannot be done because the purchase already exceeds the materiality threshold.

2. Your company purchases a chair worth $100, which has an expected lifetime of ten years. Normally, the matching principle will dictate that you record the chair as an asset that will depreciate over the next ten years. However, since the materiality principle exists, you do not have to record depreciation of the chair at $10 over each of the ten years because the sum of money is very small and it will not affect the way investors see your company.

Keep in mind that the materiality principle should not be abused. Taking the last example above, if your company purchases 100 chairs and another 100 tables worth $500 each, the matter will have to be treated differently because the sum of money and the depreciation of those products will affect the company's statements and will be noticeable to anyone reading them.

The Consistency Principle

T he consistency principle (or the consistency restraint, if we have to name it more correctly) is another important principle to consider when doing the accounting of a company.

This accounting constraint requires you to focus on one accounting method and stick to it. So, once you decide on a principle (or set of principles) to follow in your business, you have to be consistent about this and follow it throughout all of the accounting periods your business (or the business you work for) goes through.

To better define the consistency principle, we have to underline, once again, that the generally accepted accounting principles are not *legislation* per se - but they are tightly connected to actual legislation and following them will inevitably help you adhere to the laws that are in place.

The consistency principle is no exception to the rule. Not being consistent with the principles and methods you follow in your accounting might not have direct legal implications, but it could lead to a misleading portrayal of your business in the eyes of investors and creditors, and thus, it could lead to legal ramifications.

Why Is Consistency So Important?

Accounting consistency is important for a lot of reasons, but some of the most important ones include the following:

1. It allows financial information to be comparable. When accountants use the same method from one accounting year to the next, all of their financial statements will have (more or less) the same structure. Therefore, managers, creditors, investors, bankers, and anyone who reads those financial statements can clearly analyze and compare the performance of the business over different years.

2. It allows accountants to be efficient both from a time-related point of view and from a cost-related one. Once your accountants and managers learn your chosen method, you will not have to spend time (and potentially money) for them to be trained in another method if you decide to change at a later date.

3. Auditors will actually request it. External auditors (hired by your company or by an investor, for example) want to see consistent reporting. If they spot any kind of changes in the principles you have followed, this could affect the interpretation they give financial statements - so they will require further information regarding the inconsistency.

Do You Have to Stick to the Same Rules Forever?

The main goal with the consistency principle is to help accountants make sure that all the transactions and events they record follow the same methodology from one accounting period to another.

For instance, if you have decided to follow accrual accounting, you will have to stick to this throughout all of your financial statements. Likewise, if you have decided to follow the rules of cash accounting, you will have to be consistent about this.

Furthermore, you will have to decide on whether you follow international standards or national standards as well - and you will have to stick to your choice one accounting period after another.

You cannot simply switch from one accounting method to another from one year to another. However, *you can* switch from one set of rules to another if this change is justified.

When that happens, and you absolutely have to start following a different set of rules, you should make yourself accountable for the change. You need to clearly explain the reason you have switched accounting principles and you should do this in the financial statement of the company so that anyone who reads it understands the context and the implications of your change.

The consistency principle is there because it prevents companies (and accountants) from manipulating financial statements to their advantage. This way, the business reports will remain accurate, and the information will be easy to compare and contrast when this is needed.

It is of the utmost importance that you note any changes to accounting principles followed. And it is extremely important that you do this correctly, in the spirit of full disclosure. These changes should normally be noted in the financial statement footnotes and it should all be done transparently and clearly.

Examples of How the Consistency Principle Is Used

We have also gathered some examples of how the consistency principle is used, to help you gain a better understanding of what it is and how to deal with it in the best way possible. Here they are:

1. Let's say you need to buy software for your company and it is quite expensive. Normally, you could write these down as expenses and get a tax deduction on it. However, if you do this now, you will have to do it the next year as well, regardless of whether or not you need a tax deduction that year (or if you think the software would be better amortized). Doing one thing this year and treating your expenses differently the next would come in contradiction with the consistency principle.

2. You own a small store and you use the FIFO method for your inventory (First In, First Out). Now that your business has become quite successful, your bookkeeper suggests that you switch to LIFO inventory valuing (Last In, First Out) because this would help you minimize the taxes you pay for your income. Now, this can be a tricky example - changing to LIFO would be, in theory, a justifiable reason. However, the purpose behind it is to minimize the taxes, which might be (rightfully so) on the edge between acceptable and unacceptable. Your accountant should help you make a decision in this respect so that you are covered from a legal point of view.

Let's say you have made the switch to LIFO, but now you are facing a drop in sales and you are considering going back to FIFO the next year. According to the consistency principle, this is not allowed because the reason behind the change is clearly not justifiable.

The consistency principle puts a stop to any kind of potentially odd maneuvers management and bookkeepers might want to make in order to keep their financial statement in a positive light. Plus, it makes it easier for you as an accountant or business owner as well - you can easily follow the same rules year after year, and make sure you get it right every time.

The Conservatism Principle

The conservatism principle is one of the generally accepted accounting principles that might sound downright odd to some people. However, it is extremely important to understand it and apply it in your accounting methods.

The main idea behind conservatism is that your business should be able to anticipate and record future losses, and not necessarily future gains. This principle is especially important when it comes to cases of uncertainty, as well as cases when estimates are needed. When these situations occur, you, as a bookkeeper, have to always lean towards solutions that are conservative.

Basically, the conservatism principle says that, whenever you are uncertain as to how to proceed about a transaction and how to record it, you should take the path that seems to be more conservative. Here, the term "conservative" is meant to describe the solution that provides a less favorable outcome. So, for instance, if you have to record the estimated expenses of a company, you have to record them by minimizing the profits, not by estimating the maximum gains.

As a rule of thumb, whenever there is uncertainty about future losses, you are bound by the conservatism principle to record them. If, however, uncertainty occurs when it comes to future gains, you should not record it (if there is absolute certainty about that gain, though, you *should* record it).

Why Follow the Conservatism Principle?

The main purpose of the conservatism principle, as in the case of all generally accepted accounting principles, is to provide useful financial data to whoever is bound to read them (investors, bankers, creditors, and so on). Overestimating financial information might lead to an error that is prejudicial to a potential investor, for example. Underestimating it, however, will not lead to unfortunate situations and it will not sway the investor's decision on the positive side of things.

The conservatism principle is very much connected to the matching principle and to the revenue recognition principle according to which revenues and expenses have to be recognized when they happen. If, however, there is doubt over whether or not they will happen, you will have to rely on the conservatism principle and recognize revenues when they actually happen and expenses when they are reasonably near.

Auditors are very keen on their clients' following of the conservatism principle, precisely because a non-conservative entry in financial statements would provide unreliable data.

The conservatism principle lies at the very basis of the market rule (or lower of cost rule), according to which you should always record inventory with the lower value of its acquisition cost or the market value it has at the moment.

Unlike with other principles, the conservatism principle tends to be against taxing authorities. The reason this happens is because when the conservatism principle is employed, the results of financial statements is lower - and therefore, the taxable income itself is lower.

Examples of How the Conservatism Principle Works

The conservatism principle does require a bit of knowledge and common sense from the side of the accountant - in the sense that bookkeepers have to err on the least positive outcome and they have to know when this is needed.

Here are some examples of how the conservatism principle might be applied:

1. Your company has to face a patent lawsuit. Another competitor has sued you for patent infringement and they expect to win the lawsuit, with a pretty significant settlement. There is a pretty big chance they will win - but this is not certain, so your competitor will not record the gain as part of their official statement, precisely because there is a chance they might not see this happen (or not on the terms they foresee). Recording the gain at a maximum value would influence the people reading the financial statements, and it could mislead them should the company lose the lawsuit or win the lawsuit with a smaller settlement.

   On the other side, you, as the one who shows higher odds of losing the lawsuit, should record the loss in the footnotes of your official financial statements because this is the most conservative way to treat the situation from an accounting point of view. If you expect to have to pay a settlement in the future, the users of your financial statements have the right to know this because it will influence whether or not they invest in or they credit your company.

2. You own a record company and you have to release a new album soon. Still, you are not certain if you owe royalties to certain artists who recorded the album - mostly because of the contracts you signed with them and because of the legal disputes associated with them. In this situation, you would be required by the conservatism principle to actually record this situation as a contingent liability, in the footnotes of your financial statements.

3. You own a retail company and offer your customers a line of credit to make purchases. If the collection staff of your company recognizes some of your receivables have a 5% bad debt percentage (because of it happening before in the same situation), but your sales team thinks the bad debt percentage is higher (because the industry sales have dropped), you will have to lean towards the sales team's opinion when you create the allowance for doubtful accounts.

Finally, please bear in mind that the conservatism principle is all about playing it safe or, in terms that are even more down to earth, being *pessimistic*. You have to assume the worst: the losses will be incurred and the revenues might not happen, and this should be reflected on financial statements.

Keep in mind that you should not use this principle to *always* record the lowest possible earnings, but only when doubts are considerable over whether or not a loss or revenue might happen! In the end, the conservatism principle is a guideline. As mentioned above, accountants have to use their better judgment to evaluate these kinds of situations and record a company's transactions using the information they have.

The Cost Principle

The cost principle (or the cost constraint, to be more correct) is the last of the officially-recognized generally accepted accounting principles - but not in any way the least important one.

We have just briefly touched upon a concept similar to the cost principle in this book. Earlier, we said that when the costs of abiding by generally accepted accounting principles are too high, accountants have the possible option of omitting them.

The cost principle, also known as the cost/benefit principle or the cost/benefit constraint, states that the cost of providing information in your financial statements should be compared to the benefits of providing that information.

Now, this is a pretty tricky concept to grasp, precisely because it could lead to accountants and management to be tempted to omit certain negative information from their statements, stating that the information was too expensive to research and put together, as compared to the benefits of doing it.

It is, however, extremely important that you understand this constraint. Together with the materiality constraint, they lie at the very foundation of both generally accepted accounting principles and the constraints associated with them.

The cost benefit principle was not always followed. In the past, accountants informally tried to create some sort of balance between the cost of providing information and the practicality of doing it. However, today, a lot of businesses apply the cost benefit constraint - so they analyze the benefits of providing certain types of information in their financial statement and measure it against the cost of doing it.

The Issue with the Cost Principle

The cost/benefit principle is, like all generally accepted accounting principles, simple in theory. But it can get very complicated when you go in-depth and try to apply it to real life situations.

The cost part of the cost benefit principle is easy. You pretty much just have to analyze the costs of collecting, researching, putting together, processing, analyzing, storing, auditing, and sharing data.

When it comes to the benefit part of the same principle, however, things can get very tricky, because it is difficult to quantify it. For instance, if the information you want to provide an investor will offer them the chance for an accurate assessment of the company's financial situation, this is clearly a benefit and the information should be included. However, it is difficult to assign an actual value (numerical value, for that matter) to this benefit.

This entire issue makes the application of the cost/benefit principle a judgment call on the side of the accountants handling the situation. At all times, the concept of transparency should be applied, though - which means that you should not use the cost/benefit principle in an abusive way, to maneuver financial statements to the company's major advantage.

Is the Cost Principle Applied at All Times?

No, the cost benefit constraint is not to be applied on all types of financial reports. The ones the cost benefit principle applies to are very clearly stipulated in the accounting standards - and in all of the situations excluded from that list, all of the financial data should be reported regardless of what the costs associated with this might be.

In reality, very few types of information are actually expensive to acquire and this means that there is a very small number of situations when accountants are allowed to actually forego and avoid reporting a situation.

The cost benefit constraint is there to help bookkeepers and management keep everything transparent *and* efficient for the company. It is, however, one of the generally accepted accounting principles you are not very likely to use very often, precisely because it is very well-constrained itself as well. Use it cautiously and always check with the official accounting standards when in doubt!

Alternatives to GAAP
and Everything They Imply

In the beginning of the book, we were discussing the fact that, although rule-based, generally accepted accounting principles method have their flaws and that they are not always useful for companies who want to provide the best and most reliable information to financial statement readers.

Within the body of generally accepted accounting principles, there is, however, a pretty fascinating world flourishing: the alternative GAAP. Or, in other words, rules and guidelines that have derived from the GAAP, extending their force beyond that, and based on real-life situations that have pushed accountants into going farther with their interpretation of a system that was, at least initially, conceived to be *uninterpretable.*

As a disclaimer, this chapter is going to be a long and winding one. We have thus far exposed the main generally accepted accounting principles and helped you understand what they really stand for.

From here on, we will dive deeper into the exceptions to those rules, how they happen, and what solutions there might be for them.

Keep in mind, though: the following subchapters of this *Accounting Principles* book do not serve as a day to day guide in accounting for companies who are large, public, or simply fit into the GAAP in terms of how they create their financial statements.

The following subchapters have two main purposes: to show that although rule-based, the GAAP allows for additional concepts to be added to the appendix body of generally accepted accounting principles AND to show you just how madly fascinating accounting can be when we go beyond entries, numbers, subtractions, and additions.

So, without further ado, let us proceed.

Understanding How the Standards Are Set

In every country, there is a body of accounting professionals that have the authority to select, draw, and establish the main accounting principles bookkeepers of all kinds must follow when preparing the financial statements within that given country.

Normally, you'd say *yes, this is the right way to do it. There must be a standardization committee in charge of establishing what must or mustn't be done.*

And you'd be right.

But going deeper than that will reveal a pretty big issue: how is that board of specialists itself being set and how does it operate?

Should the government be in charge of it, or should a body of private-sector professionals be dealing with this?

Should there be any degree of flexibility in the way they establish the rules and in the way they are applied, or should this be uniform at all times? What is the most efficient way to measure the economic results of a company's activities?

Should it all be rule-based or principle-based?

These are all important questions - questions that are still very much debated (as I have shown in the beginning of this book, for example, when I briefly touched upon the advantages and disadvantages of both the rule-based and the principle-based systems).

In the United States, the US Congress is the absolute, ultimate authority when it comes to establishing the acceptable accounting principles in America. This task is normally delegated to the SEC (Securities and Exchange Commission), which is a federal government agency. In their own turn, the SEC generally accepts everything the FASB (the Financial Accounting Standards Board) deems as acceptable accounting principles.

On the surface, the standard setting process in the US resides in the private sector. In reality, however, both the SEC and FASB communicate on every issue that might arise. The very proof of this is that FASB founded the EITF (Emerging Issues Task Force) when it was asked by the SEC to do so. This task force's purpose is to deal with any kind of reporting issues in cases where FASB has not issued any kind of statement just yet.

For a bit more background, we will reinstate the fact that most accounting firms in the US have some sort of flexibility in choosing their accounting principles - to some extent, of course. While in some instances the specific situation associated with a transaction a company has to record dictates the accounting method that is to be used, there are also cases when a wide degree of flexibility is applied, allowing companies to choose alternative methods.

"Constrained flexibility" is frequently used to describe accounting principles in the US On the one hand, the government recognizes that their goal (raising tax revenues) is different from the goal of their users who read financial reports (understanding them at their true value and being able to compare and contrast them). This is why the SEC and FASB have been assigned with the task of setting the standards.

When they select accounting principles, FASB takes two main elements into consideration: making deductions from all general principles *and* detailing the rules when this is needed.

It is important to note that their main methodology does not always give FASB the best and clearest guidance when it comes to the alternative methods the accountants might have to use when recording a transaction or event.

On top of this, lobbying companies might also incline FASB towards one side or another, arguing that they cannot apply certain methods in a cost-efficient way (which comes in contradiction to the cost benefit principle of GAAP itself). Furthermore, they sometimes claim that using generally accepted accounting principles will eventually disrupt decisions taken within their company and their capital markets as well.

There were instances when, under the pressure of lobbyists, FASB decided on specific standards, only to come back to them when regulators and academics flagged the standards as unethical or unprofessional for accountants.

This proves that the entire standard setting process in the United States (in accounting, and, most likely, in many other areas) is heavily influenced by politics and in itself, holds a political nature as well.

Governmental agencies in other countries too have a very powerful role in establishing the accounting standards to be used in those countries (such as Germany, Japan, or France, for example). However, the different ways in which these different standards have been set, changed, and influenced has led to accounting standards that are quite different from the United States.

As shown here, the accounting standard setting process is far from perfect. It has its flaws, and it has mishaps as well. However, because multiple institutions and professionals are watching over the entire standard setting process, it is far more unlikely that anything will slip through, allowing companies to make a grave error (intentional or not).

On the one hand, there is the governmental agency guarding over everything the private body does. On the other hand, there are the external professionals who might trigger a red flag when lobbyists push towards standards that would only benefit specific businesses, and not the entirety of the business community or the government in any way (e.g. standards that would allow for too much leeway in tax deductions would not have a long life).

The process of setting accounting standards is long and winding - and this is a perfect explanation of *why* it takes so long to come up with a body of accounting standards that is at least somewhat universally accepted.

Communication, in this sense, is being made - and with so many businesses expanding across the borders of the countries they were initially founded in, it makes perfect sense that an agreement will be reached - if not soon, then *at some point* in the future.

How Are the Alternatives to GAAP Used?

As mentioned before, most of the time, GAAP and IFRS standards are the best ways for businesses to do their bookkeeping and financial reporting. These standards are all there for a purpose: to help businesses make sure that they all play by the same rules and create the kind of financial statements that can be easily followed, compared, and analyzed.

As also shown before, these accounting standards can pose issues sometimes - and most often, this happens with small and medium-sized businesses (SMBs). The debates on alternative accounting standards and the results these debates have led to have, however, helped SMBs a lot in this respect.

In fact, institutions have gone so far as to develop a set of alternative standards called Other Comprehensive Basis of Accounting (created by the American Institute of Certified Public Accountants and the International Accounting Standards Board). This newer set of guidelines and rules offers small and medium-sized businesses standards that are easier to adopt on their end. On the investors' and lenders' end, more and more of them become accustomed to and accept these new standards.

To put into perspective, the IFRS for SMBs is more simplified than the US GAAP. By comparison, the first has 230 pages, while the latter has no less than 20,000 pages of information.

The main challenge of these new (or alternative) standards is for both accountants and the finance community to learn how to adapt the methods that are currently used to these new standards. While in many countries, these standards are already deemed legitimate and acceptable, there is still much debate over whether or not everyone should move to the simpler, more concise standards.

It makes sense why so many have doubts. Until now, with some exceptions (some of which have grown into fully-fledged financial scandals), GAAP and extensive sets of standards have proved useful. So it is perfectly natural for all the players on the other side of the fence (bankers, investors, credit-rating agencies, and so on) would be wary in the case of a an oversimplification of the standards already set in place - mostly because it could lead to severe gaps and misinterpretations in the companies' financial statements.

On the other hand, a separate set of standards for small and medium businesses means that the accounting for their goodwill, investments, business combinations and other similar issues would be more simplified.

Given the explanation we have given in the previous subchapter on the intricacies of the standard-setting process, it is likely that quite a lot of time will pass before special standards for SMBs will be actually accepted at a unanimous level. It would, however, help these small and medium-sized businesses grow at a better, healthier pace, focusing on actual growth, rather than reporting standards, while still being able to access the help provided by investors and creditors.

Are Alternative GAAP Methods Misleading?

This is, by far, one of the single most important questions when it comes to alternatives to generally accepted accounting principles. In the end, all of the accounting principles exist with the sole purpose of making financial reporting more transparent, especially for users of the financial reports.

Alternative GAAP methods might be, thus, considered to be misleading in some situations. However, further talk needs to be done on this topic, especially since alternative GAAP methods and adjacent GAAP rules might actually prove useful in a wide variety of contexts.

To understand how these GAAP alternatives might be misleading, we will first dive into some of the most commonly used methods:

1. Earnings before interest and taxes (also known as EBIT)

2. Earnings before interest, taxes, depreciation, and amortization (EBITDA)

3. Adjusted earnings

In general, all methods that are not comprised by the GAAP are considered to be alternative. These methods are used when generally accepted accounting principles cannot convey nuances that might help financial statement readers gain a deeper understanding of a company's financial status and where it goes.

When companies feel the need to supplement (and this is a keyword!) the GAAP financial reporting with alternative methods, they often use it outside of financial statements per se, to describe items that are non-recurrent, but might affect the way a potential investor and creditor sees the company.

Non-GAAP methods are not standardized, so it is of the utmost importance for companies to have a very well-established set of controls and procedures that will help them make sure these measures are properly and accurately disclosed. These controls and procedures also help companies comply with the rules and regulations enforced by the SEC.

To establish these controls and procedures, companies must turn their attention to the following areas:

1. Compliance. All non-GAAP methods have to comply with the rules, regulations, and guidance enforced by the SEC.

2. Consistency. All non-GAAP methods must be presented in a consistent way, each accounting period. All the adjustments that

are non-GAAP should be evaluated and applied in an appropriate and consistent way.

3. Data reliability. All the data used for the non-GAAP measures must be reliable at all times.

4. Calculation accuracy. All non-GAAP measures have to be flawlessly calculated.

5. Transparency. When non-GAAP measures are being used, they have to be fully, clearly, and unambiguously disclosed.

6. Management review. If non-GAAP methods must be applied, they have to be reviewed and confirmed by the management of the company, to ensure that they are appropriate.

7. Audit and management monitoring. When non-GAAP measures are used, they are fully disclosed, and their disclosure is closely monitored by the senior management of the company, as well as by the auditing committee.

How to Disclose Non-GAAP Measures

When your company has to use non-standard accounting methods, they have to be fully and transparently disclosed in financial statement appendixes.

One of the most important parts of this process is about involving the management of the company in it. In some situations, this only needs to be done with a disclosure committee, in other situations, it has to be done with the audit committee, and in other situations, it has to be done with the involvement of both of these committees.

SEC regulations state that all companies should consider creating a written policy to describe the nature of the adjustments to GAAP that are allowed and the actual non-GAAP measures to be used. Furthermore, companies should also explain the changes they have made that will influence inputs, calculations, and adjustments.

A disclosure committee should assist the CEO, CFO, and the audit committee in creating and monitoring disclosures - including, but not limited to non-GAAP methods that might be used. In most cases, the disclosure committee is formed out of management - but in some cases, companies might allow the disclosure committee to function as a sub-branch of the board.

Such a policy might describe any or all of the following:

1. A qualitative description of the adjustments made that are non-recurring;

2. A quantitative description of the thresholds at which any kind of income or expenses have to be evaluated to determine if they should or shouldn't be included in the non-GAAP adjustments.

As you can see, even when non-GAAP methods are used, they have to be internally regulated and they also have to be fully disclosed to external readers of the financial statements.

Can the use of non-GAAP measures still be confusing and maybe even intentionally misleading in this case?

Well, yes. Given that the drafting and the disclosure of these methods happen internally, they could be used to put a company in a better light than it actually is. The SEC had been closely monitoring the use of non-GAAP methods since 2016, and an internal task force has been created with this purpose.

Whenever possible, try to avoid non-GAAP measures - they can be misleading indeed, and they can be very complicated to draft as a disclosure statement. They can, at times, prove useful as well - so, again, it is all a matter of judgment calls you have to make as an accountant.

Contemporary Debate Against Non-GAAP

The Enron scandal happened more than 17 years ago but to date, it lingers as one of the most prominent and notable financial scandals of the United States of America. Back then, the SEC urged for the creation of rules for non-GAAP measures.

A little over two years ago, in 2016, the lack of regulation for non-GAAP methods was put under scrutiny once again - this time, in a Valeant Pharmaceuticals case that reminded the whole world of the Enron situation at the beginning of the 2000s. As with Enron, Valeant was not fully honest in their financial statements - and they are paying dearly for this.

On the surface, many things have changed since the Enron scandal that urged American authorities toward better regulations. However, the Valeant Pharmaceuticals case proves that there is still a lot of leeway and that companies still practice dubious financial statement methods, most of which are at least somewhat fueled by the non-GAAP methods.

You might be tempted to think that not a lot of companies do the same - but in reality, even companies that abide by the generally accepted accounting principles still find loopholes they can use to manipulate the numbers. Studies show that this happens a lot more frequently than we might believe.

In themselves, non-GAAP methods are not *inherently bad*. Their existence is allowed precisely because GAAP can be, at times, flawed. In the hands of irresponsible and dishonest companies and executives, however, these non-GAAP methods can turn into a real tool of manipulation and misinformation - and yes, this hurts investors *a lot*.

Take, for example, the issue of performance-based bonuses. They have been tax deductible for more than twenty years (nearly thirty) now - and companies frequently compensate executives this way. Most of the time, however, reporting these compensations is tightly knit to non-GAAP metrics that are created in a way that executives always reach their targets.

Consequently, executives are very tempted to maneuver non-GAAP methods in any way they can, so that they can reach their target. For instance, if a company reports restructuring as a non-recurring charge, this would be done through a non-GAAP method. However, regulation is unclear as to how many times this can be done - so if the company does it for two years in a row, there should be something suspicious there (because those charges can hardly be considered as "non-recurring", given that they have happened for so many years in a row).

Similar tactics are used all over the financial world. While we are not saying that these methods are inefficient, we are saying that they are very unethical and that, once the problem explodes, it can lead to severe legal issues for you as an individual helping with the manipulation and for your company as well.

How Common Accounting Concepts Connect to GAAP and Alternatives to GAAP

As established in the first chapters of this book, generally accepted accounting principles are rules that have to be followed by the accounting community (in this case, because these are the US GAAP, the rules have to be followed by accountants in the United States of America).

Up until now, we have gone through the most important rules of accounting - generally accepted accounting principles - and described their purpose and their use.

To help you gain an even better understanding of what these rules are all about, we will now put them through the lens of some of the most essential accounting terms:

Revenue Recognition

It is important to know when revenue should be recognized, because, according to the basics of different types of accounting, this happens at different times, influencing when it should be entered onto balance sheets.

Here are the instances when revenue recognition should occur:

1. When goods are sold or services are rendered (in accrual accounting);

2. When cash is collected - either through installments or through the cost-recovery-first method (in cash accounting);

3. When the production or construction of a product begins (in the percentage-of-completion method of accounting, usually applied in the case of long-term contracts);

4. When a customer's return time expires (if your business allows customers to return products in a given amount of time after purchase).

In general, recognizing revenue at the time of production will lead to reports with a large cumulative income and assets - and this is closely followed by the recognition of revenue when a sale happens.

It is worth mentioning, however, that the revenue recognition model that produces the largest earnings will vary a lot, depending on the accounting period, and the specificities of a business in general.

Generally speaking, companies that are on a growing path will report the largest earnings when they record their revenues when production or construction happens. Companies that are on a decline, however, will report the largest earnings when they make their recognition at the time of cash collection. Steady firms (that don't grow or decline) will usually report more or less the same earnings, accounting period after accounting period.

Please note that regardless of the revenue recognition method and accounting method you have chosen, this will only affect the timing and not the amount of revenue itself. Does this have an impact on financial statements? Yes, somewhat - in the sense that if your statements are released right after a surge in sales, they might not be 100% accurate. Accounting standards do seem to allow this, however - and accountants have quite a lot of freedom when it comes to choosing their accounting method.

In some cases, recognizing the revenue when it happens (e.g. when goods or services are sold, such as in accrual accounting) is the better option. However, if you run a company that will conduct operations over the course of multiple years to deliver one project (e.g a construction company), you will find that the percentage-of-completion method suits them better.

Uncollectible Accounts

This concept has been touched upon in our previous chapters - but we want to dive a little deeper into it because it can be very complex. Of course, this is the kind of concept that would take an entire separate book (to say the least) to explain - but we will try to provide you with a little more information here, for the purpose of a better understanding of accounting principles in general.

A firm can recognize an expense as uncollectible in two moments: the accounting period when it recognizes the revenue (such as in the allowance method) or in the accounting period when the discovery that the collection of specific accounts cannot happen is made (such as in the direct write-off method).

The first method will usually result in the smallest earnings and assets on the balance sheet. The reason this happens is because it recognizes the bad debt earlier than the other method mentioned above.

The method showing the largest cumulative assets and earnings depends on each business and the specificities of their operations. However, it is very important to note that GAAP requires accountants to use the allowance method if the uncollectible amounts are predictable. At the same time, however, the income tax legislation in the United States requires firms to use the direct write-off method when it comes to tax reporting.

Inventories

In general, companies report their inventories using the lower side of the acquisition cost or market value. However, there are instances when a company cannot or simply doesn't want to specifically identify which of the goods in its inventory it has sold - and in such situations, a cost flow assumption is made.

There are multiple types of cost flow assumption models - such as FIFO, LIFO, or weighted average. IASB will generally prefer the FIFO or weighted average method because they tend to be more accurate. For instance, in the case of FIFO, the largest earnings and assets of a company's valuations will be recorded when the acquisition costs increase - and the lowest earnings and assets will be reported when the acquisition costs decrease.

LIFO, on the other hand, works the exact opposite way, showing the smallest earnings and assets when the acquisition cost is boosted and the highest earnings when they decline. This makes LIFO the least conservative method of doing inventory, and thus it makes it less GAAP-compliant as well.

Generally speaking, if only very small changes in acquisition costs occur, the earnings and assets valuations will not be reported much differently. However, the more rapid the rate of inventory turnover is, the more you will reduce the difference between the three methods of cost flow assumptions.

Last, but not least, it is important to note that in most cases, accountants have quite a lot of freedom in selecting the types of cost flow assumption methods they want to use. It is also worth mentioning that in the United States, firms are obliged to use LIFO in financial reporting if they are using it for tax reporting as well.

Depreciable Assets

Machinery, equipment, as well as other depreciable assets have a special way of being treated from an accounting point of view.

Companies are allowed to depreciate fixed assets using different methods: the straight line, the declining balance, the sum of the year's digits method, or the units of production method.

In some parts of the world, tax reporting has been playing a very important role in setting the acceptable accounting standards (such as Germany or France, for example). In those countries, firms are more inclined to use accelerated depreciation methods for the purpose of financial reporting.

In other countries, however, where different accounting methods are used for tax reporting (such as the UK and the USA, for instance), accountants are more inclined to use the straight-line method. This method will normally provide the largest earnings and asset valuations, while the sum of the years' digits is next in line from this point of view.

When the acquisition costs of any of the depreciable assets are at least somewhat stable and when the companies maintain their investment levels in these products or services, the depreciation methods mentioned before will produce similar balance sheets.

Accountants are allowed to use different estimates when it comes to the life expectancy of depreciable assets - mostly because the intensity of the use and the maintenance/repair policies could affect the age at which these assets are considered depreciated.

In most parts of the world, income tax laws do not require conformity between the different tax methods used to report depreciable assets. There are, however, some exceptions to the norm.

Asset impairment is a concept adjacent to asset depreciation. All firms have the obligation to test their depreciable assets when an event suggests that their estimation of the fair value of the asset has declined. For instance, if your company has 50 laptops it has depreciated over the next 5 years, but two of them break unexpectedly, you should consider an asset impairment evaluation.

In the US, this compares the undiscounted cash flow that was initially estimated from the asset and their book value. If the latter exceeds the first, the asset impairment is official. The firm is then supposed to measure the impairment loss by comparing the fair value (market value or the present value of the expected cash flow associated with that asset) and the book value. The excess amount resulting from this calculation is considered to be the amount of the impairment loss.

Leases

If you run a company that uses property rights acquired on lease, you can record this in multiple ways. You can record the lease as an asset (and thus, be able to amortize it through the capital lease method) or you can recognize the lease transaction only when the company uses the asset, making payments each accounting period (and this is called the "operating lease method").

If you are the lessor in this situation, you can use the same methods. You can use the capital lease method (in which you set up the rights to receive the lease payments at the beginning of the lease) or you can use the operating lease method (in which you recognize the lease when you have already become entitled to receive the lease payments each accounting period).

Each lease situation is different and the two methods described above provide advantages and disadvantages, depending on the particular situation. In general, both the lessor and the lessee will use the same method for their lease contract, so that they can apply the same criteria from a capital vs. operating point o view. At the same time, however, the lessor and the lessee don't have to coordinate their accounting methods as well.

As you can see, all the aforementioned situations described in this subchapter are based on basic generally accepted accounting principles - but the situations and the complexity of the concepts has determined that new, adjacent rules should be applied.

These are just some examples - in reality, the alternatives to GAAP can get even harsher and they can produce even more intricate situations. In the end, however, this is part of the beauty of accounting: it may be a discipline dealing in numbers, but it can be very complex and very much based on analysis and judgment calls as well!

Other Comprehensive Basis of Accounting

As mentioned before, the American Institute for Certified Public Accountants has developed a set of accounting standards meant for businesses who cannot (for one reason or another) comply with generally accepted accounting principles. This set of standards comes under the name of "other comprehensive basis of accounting" (or OCBOA).

The other comprehensive basis of accounting standards include rules on how financial statements should be prepared in the absence of GAAP (but based on arguments that are supported in popular specialty literature). Furthermore, these rules also include a different basis of accounting (statutory) - one that is frequently used by insurance companies to comply with the commissions of state insurance.

Preparing your financial statements under OCBOA has two main advantages:

- The result will be generally easier to understand than statements created following GAAP (which, quite frankly, can be very intricate);

- The costs associated with preparing a financial statement under OCBOA is usually significantly smaller than that of preparing a financial statement under GAAP.

OCBOA and GAAP have the same purpose: that of helping accountants produce financial statements that are transparent and clear for their users. One of the main differences between the systems is that according to the other comprehensive basis of accounting rules, cash flow statements are not required.

There is, as you would expect, quite a lot of criticism surrounding OCBOA - and one of the main points critics bring up is connected to the fact that disclosures are not properly made. Thus, specialists recommend that a very comprehensive disclosure should be made by any business that is using the other comprehensive basis of accounting rules, so that financial statement readers get a full, clean, and understandable picture of that company's financial records. Comprehensive disclosures should include all the details needed for the understanding of financial statements - including, but not limited to, the basis of accounting used, any kind of risks, uncertainties, and contingent liabilities as well.

What Is Considered OCBOA?

According to the US Statement on Auditing Standards, it can be considered as "other comprehensive basis of accounting" in any of the following situations:

- Using a statutory basis of accounting (such as in the example given above, with the basis of accounting used by insurance companies);

- Cash-basis financial statements, as well as modified-cash-basis statements too;

- Financial statements on an income tax basis;

- Any financial statements that have been produced using support from specialty literature, which is then applied throughout the entirety of the financial statement and the material items appearing in it.

There are a number of situations when OCBOA statements are preferred, for a variety of reasons. These situations include:

- Cases when a GAAP statement is not necessary because of the loan covenants;

- Cases when a GAAP statement is not needed because of regulatory circumstances;

- Cases when businesses focus on who the users of financial statements are and what they want to see from the financial statements (e.g. cases when the financial statement is required by regulatory agencies);

- Cases when the company needs to reduce the cost of financial statements and audits (as OCBOA-based statements are, as mentioned before, simpler and less expensive to produce).

It is extremely important to note the fact that, indeed, the other comprehensive basis of accounting rules are quite different from generally accepted accounting principles. They are, however, guided by a code as well. This code includes rules such as:

- All professional accounting standards are still applicable to OCBOA-based financial statements;

- There must be a disclosure of the basis of accounting needed;

- The statements must be titled in a way that draws a clear distinguishable line between them and the titles of statements created based on GAAP;

- OCBOA statements can still be audited. Furthermore, they can be compiled and reviewed as well;

- All the disclosures included in an OCBOA statement are supposed to be comparably as intricate as the ones included in a GAAP financial statement. They should be relevant, and the information provided in these disclosures should be clear and substantial;

- If a company has to modify an OCBOA rule, the modifications have to keep the OCBOA rule separate from a GAAP rule (and they should not result in an accounting rule that looks like a modified GAAP).

Although OCBOA accounting standards are generally accepted, it is better to stick to GAAP rules whenever possible, especially throughout the United States. This will help you ensure that your financial statements are fully compliant - but maybe even more importantly in the long run, it will help you make sure that your investors and creditors can actually read, compare, and analyze your statements at their true value, and provide you with the help you need based on an honest view of your company's financial status.

The International Financial Reporting Standards

This entire book has been dedicated to generally accepted accounting principles - mostly because, well, these are the standards used in the United States (and thus, the standards you would use as a US business too).

However, international financial reporting standards are also important to know - not only because they provide a clear understanding of how accounting itself works, but because the US might move towards this approach as well. Regardless of whether or not this happens, though, knowing the IFRS standards is useful for all accountants.

Without further ado, let's proceed and dive into this topic a little deeper.

How Are the IFRS Defined?

The international financial reporting standards (IFRS) are a set of standards created and monitored by the IFRS Foundation, as well as by IABS (International Accounting Standards Board). The main purpose of these International Financial Reporting Standards is to provide a common set of standards and a common language for businesses across different countries.

International shareholding has also had a pretty heavy influence on the development of IFRS, and the fact that a lot of companies do business in several countries has played a role as well.

IFRS is gradually replacing the national accounting standards present in countries around the world. These rules (or, as we have established in the beginning of the book, *principles*) are meant to be followed by accountants so that users of financial statements from different countries can understand, compare and contrast them.

Initially, the IFRS system was created to harmonize accounting methods used in the European Union. However, the value of this system was quickly adopted around the world as well.

In theory, the IFRS set of standards would create cohesiveness for the international accounting community. In practice, however, the IFRS has faced quite a lot of criticism - such as the fact that it has not been adopted in the US (one of the largest players in the international business market), or that it does not work well in hyperinflationary economies - such as Zimbabwe.

What Are the Main IFRS Principles?

Unlike generally accepted accounting principles used in the United States of America, the IFRS standards are a set of principles - not rules. This has been explained in the beginning of the book as well: GAAP sets very clear rules accountants should follow, while IFRS sets guidelines to help accountants adhere to legislation and good practices at an international level.

The main objective behind international financial reporting standards is to provide a uniform way of presenting financial statements around the world. As also discussed in the book thus far, financial statements are a representation of the financial status of a business entity, created with the purpose of providing information to external and internal readers. What a financial statement should show is how the resources of a company have been used by management in terms of financial performance and cash flow.

The general features of the international financial reporting standards include the following:

1. Fair and faithful presentation. This feature is all about the honesty with which a company produces their financial statements, how they mirror their transactions and the effects of these transactions in these statements, and how they portray events and conditions associated with the transactions in their financial statements.

2. Going concern. This concept is also found in generally accepted accounting principles, and it means the same thing: financial statements are made on the assumption that the business will continue its operations and that it will not liquidate.

3. Accrual accounting. In the case of GAAP, accrual accounting is normally the accounting method suggested (but companies are still allowed to use other types of accounting methods, according to their needs). The use of accrual accounting extends into the IFRS as well - and this means that both revenue and expenses should be recognized as such when they satisfy a given set of criteria (as elaborated in the Framework of IFRS).

4. Materiality and the aggregation of it. The name of this concept is similar to the materiality principle of the GAAP - but it is very important to note that they are not the same in nature. In the IFRS spectrum, materiality and aggregation refer to the fact that every material class of items that are similar should be presented separately. Items that are not similar in nature should also be presented separately.

5. Offsetting. In general, offsetting is forbidden according to IFRS (where "offsetting" is defined as the cancellation of an entry, without an entry that is equal in nature and opposite in meaning). When certain conditions are met, however, the IFRS allows for offsetting. For instance, when doing the accounting for any of the benefit liabilities described in IAS 19, you are allowed to offset your entries.

6. Frequency. According to IFRS, companies should release financial statements on a minimum frequency of one per year. Internal financial statements are also allowed on a more frequent basis, but they should also be IFRS compliant as well.

7. Comparative data. The international financial reporting standards also require companies to present comparative

information and place their financial statements in comparison to preceding accounting periods for all amounts reported in the current statement. Of course, this should be done only if it is relevant and if it provides readers with a better, more in-depth understanding of the financial status of a company.

8. Consistency. The presentation and the classification of the different items comprised in a financial statement should be the same from one accounting period to another. There are exceptions to this, however. For instance, if the operations of the business have changed in nature, the reporting can be done differently. Also, if an IFRS standard requires a change from the company, they should comply and apply that change.

All in all, financial statements that abide with international financial reporting standards should have six qualities: relevance and faithful representation (fundamental qualities), comparability, verifiability, timeliness and understandability (enhancing qualities).

In many ways, the IFRS standards are similar to the US generally accepted accounting principles. There are, however, differences in nuance that prevent the two from merging (or from the US adopting international financial reporting standards).

Differences between GAAP and IFRS

The main differences between generally accepted accounting principles and international financial reporting standards include the following:

1. One is local (such as the US GAAP), while the other is global. Although IFRS standards have not been unanimously accepted

around the world, more and more countries are dropping their own accounting standardization systems and adopting the IFRS.

2. One is rule-based and the other one is principle-based. This has been discussed in more detail in the beginning of our book. There is a major difference in perception and status between the two sets of standards, and this is one of the main reasons the USA cannot move to accept the international system (not yet, at least).

3. Development costs. While in the case of GAAP, development costs have to be added as expenses in the year they occur, in the case of IFRS, they can be capitalized too.

4. The inventory methods that are allowed are very different. In the case of GAAP, companies can use LIFO if they have to do inventory estimates (or at least that is the recommended method). In the case of IFRS, LIFO is not allowed at all because it does not accurately depict the flow of inventory and the results are very low in terms of income levels.

5. Inventory write-down reversal. Tracking inventory is not the only matter that's different in GAAP and IFRS - the way inventory write-down reversals happen is different too. According to GAAP, when the market value of an asset grows, the amount of the write-down must not be reversed. In IFRS, however, this can be reversed.

6. Income statements. When it comes to IFRS, unusual items are usually included in the income statement and not segregated. However, in GAAP, they are separated from the net income and shown below this section.

7. Intangible assets. As discussed previously in this book, intangible assets cannot be actually measured - and as such, they are not considered valid under GAAP. Being a principle-based system, however, the IFRS does take into account if an asset will show any kind of future benefit from an economic point of view, assessing its value this way.

These are just some of the elements that differentiate generally accepted accounting principles from international financial reporting standards. Although the main purpose behind both of these systems is to keep accountants and companies in check and to provide them with a guide on how to make sure they abide by the legislation in action, there are drastic differences between the two systems.

Who Uses International Financial Reporting Standards?

In the United States of America, international financial reporting standards are only used by non-domestic SEC registrants. All of the companies registered domestically are meant to use GAAP, generally accepted accounting principles. By comparison, there are about 500 non-domestic companies registered at SEC - and nearly four times more domestic companies registered at the same institution.

This does not mean that knowing the IFRS is not useful for you as an accountant in the USA - especially if your company is doing business with external companies, that might be using IFRS for their financial reports. In these cases, extensive knowledge of both standard systems is needed on both ends, so that the best and most compliant solutions are found.

So, leaving aside the non-domestic companies relying on the IFRS for their financial statements, what other places use this system? Here is a list of some of the most important countries and unions that have agreed to abide by international financial reporting standards thus far:

1. The European Union. This is where the IFRS started, so it makes sense that they would adhere to this system of reporting. Currently, there are 28 countries in the EU (most of them being located in Western Europe, with some of them in Central and Central-Eastern Europe).

2. Gulf Cooperation Council. Currently, there are 7 countries in the GCC: Saudi Arabia, The United Arab Emirates, Kuwait, Qatar, Bahrain, Oman and Yemen.

3. Russia. They started coordinating their national accounting standards with IFRS in 1998.

4. Australia. They use a somewhat modified version of IFRS, which they call "Australian equivalents to IFRS" or "A-IFRS". Previously to this, they used a system that was more similar to the American GAAP.

5. Brazil. At the moment, Brazil uses IFRS for companies with publicly traded securities, as well as financial institutions with securities that are not publicly traded.

6. India. Starting in 2016, India has demanded that IFRS be implemented in a phased manner.

7. Japan. They announced in 2011 that they will adopt IFRS standards, but that there needs to be a 5-7 year period of preparations for companies, and that US GAAP can continue to

be used after the end of 2016. They will, however, switch to IFRS soon.

Aside from these countries, international financial reporting standards are also applied in the following locations: Ghana, South Korea, Hong Kong, Malaysia, Pakistan, Singapore, Chile, Philippines, Turkey, Montenegro, Nepal, Taiwan, and Zimbabwe.

In some of these countries (such as Zimbabwe), criticism has been made as to whether or not IFRS standards are a good solution - mostly because the hyperinflationary economy of these countries is not deemed suitable for the application of international financial reporting standards.

Currently, approximately 120 countries use the IFRS system. In some parts of the world, international financial reporting standards are not fully applied yet. In other parts of the world, these standards have been adopted for a long time.

In the United States, as mentioned before, the IFRS system is used only by foreign companies that have been registered at the SEC.

The urgency of aligning all accounting standards of the world becomes even more stringent as more and more companies do business overseas and across borders. Even more so, with international investors of all kinds looking to put their money into companies outside of their country of residence, the standardization of accounting rules around the world will continue to become increasingly important.

Test Your Knowledge!

As mentioned in the beginning, this book is not meant to be an in-depth manual for accountants who are already experienced at what they do.

It is, in the end, meant to have an informational purpose for accountants at the beginning of their road.

Although comprehensive, the information provided here only dips its toes into the sea of information about accounting principles and rules (be them GAAP, non-GAAP, OCBOA, or IFRS).

I hope this book has proved useful in explaining some of the basic concepts behind the large (and sometimes unstable) field of accounting principles.

So, to help you test what you have learned, I have put together a short test covering the basic concepts and examples we have touched upon in this book. There is no grading on this test - you can simply use it to revise the information you have read through, so that you can proceed on your path to understanding the in-depth intricacies of accounting principles.

The answers are at the end of the test but I do advise you, however, to try and search for them in the book, rather than jumping right to the answer.

Happy testing!

Questions:

1. In the United States, accounting standards are principle-based:

    a. Yes;

    b. No;

    c. Only some;

2. The generally accepted accounting principles are not rules per se, but guidelines into how accountants are supposed to create financial statements:

    a. No, generally accepted accounting principles are actual rules;

b. Yes, they are principles to guide accountants, not strict rules;

c. Neither, nor: some of the principles are rules, while others are principles;

3. There is virtually no difference between principle-based accounting and rule-based accounting:

a. Indeed, there is a difference based on terminology only;

b. No, the two are very different concepts;

c. Yes, there are differences, but they are very small.

4. In the United States, all companies (external or internal) have to abide by the GAAP rules:

a. Yes;

b. No;

c. Only domestic companies have to abide by GAAP rules.

5. IFRS rules are an option in the US for domestic companies:

a. Yes;

b. No;

c. Only under certain circumstances.

6. There are 10 generally accepted accounting constraints officially accepted by FASB:

   a. Yes;

   b. No, there are 5 constraints under GAAP;

   c. There are 13 constraints under GAAP.

7. FASB deals with all accounting standards around the world:

   a. Yes;

   b. No;

   c. Only with countries who have adopted IFRS.

8. Very few countries use the IFRS system, most of them relying on GAAP:

   a. Yes;

   b. No;

   c. Most countries use both IFRS and GAAP.

9. It is perfectly acceptable to use the IFRS system if it's deemed more suitable for your company

   a. Yes;

   b. No;

   c. Yes, but only as long as you use the GAAP system too.

10. Non-GAAP measures are completely illegal

    a. Yes;

    b. No, and they don't have to be disclosed;

    c. No, but they do have to be disclosed.

11. Non-GAAP measures cannot be misleading:

    a. Yes, they are very clear;

    b. No, they can be very misleading;

    c. No, they are always very misleading.

12. GAAP measures are the best type of measures because they lead to no flaws:

    a. Yes;

    b. No, and there have been major scandals related to this;

    c. No, but there is no evidence of this - only assumptions made by specialty literature professionals.

13. The IFRS system is the best system for hyperinflationary economies:

    a. Yes, but so is the GAAP;

    b. Yes, but not the GAAP;

    c. No, it has been proven to be dysfunctional in these economies.

14. No scandals have ever been created by the use of GAAP, only by the IFRS standards:

    a. Yes, GAAP has not been connected to financial scandals;

    b. No, but the GAAP scandals are minor;

    c. No, and the GAAP scandals were quite big.

15. You always have the freedom to set your own rules of accounting as long as you disclose them:

    a. Of course! Your company, your rules!

    b. Yes, but it can be tricky;

    c. Yes, but not unjustifiably.

16. GAAP rules are actual legislation:

    a. Yes, they are part of the financial laws;

    b. No, they are only connected to financial legislation;

    c. No, they are just guidelines of good practice.

17. No harm can be done if you don't follow GAAP:

    a. Your financial statements will still be easy to understand, so yes, no harm can be done;

    b. It's perfectly fine not to follow GAAP in the US;

    c. No, you have to follow GAAP (or disclose your choice of non-GAAP measures).

18. The main purpose of GAAP is to make companies pay more in taxes:

    a. Yes, the main agency monitoring GAAP is the IRS;

    b. Yes, this is the sole purpose of GAAP;

    c. No, the purpose of GAAP is to provide external financial statement users with clear, concise information that is easy to understand and compare.

19. GAAP standards are directly managed by governmental institutions (SEC):

    a. Yes;

    b. Only some of them;

    c. No.

20. GAAP standards are directly managed by private sector institutions (FASB), with no connection to governmental institutions:

    a. Yes, they are completely independent;

    b. No, FASB and governmental institutions communicate on this topic;

    c. No, GAAP standards are released by international authorities.

21. The adoption of new accounting standards is a fairly easy process and it doesn't take more than a few weeks:

    a. Yes, it is a very easy process;

    b. No, but it is a straightforward process;

    c. No, it is a process that involves many parties and can take a lot of time.

22. Small businesses and medium-sized businesses are the largest beneficiaries of the generally accepted accounting principles system:

    a. Yes;

    b. No, and they sometimes have to rely on non-GAAP measures;

    c. No, because they don't have to abide by GAAP according to US legislation.

23. You cannot, in any way, avoid using GAAP as long as your business operations happen under US jurisdiction:

    a. Yes, all businesses with business operations within the US borders have to use GAAP standards;

    b. Yes, but only domestic businesses have to abide by GAAP, SEC-registered non-domestic companies in the US can use other systems;

    c. No, GAAP is not mandatory in any way.

24. GAAP rules are not necessarily needed. In the end, each company can do whatever is best for their interest:

    a. Yes, they are just guidelines;

    b. No, GAAP rules are needed and companies have to use them;

    c. No, GAAP are needed, but companies are not obliged to use them.

25. Investors and creditors do not find GAAP rules to be helpful to them:

    a. Yes, because the purpose of GAAP is to make it hard for them to make investments;

    b. Yes, because the purpose of GAAP is to raise more taxes from businesses and investors alike;

    c. No, GAAP is meant to help investors and creditors make better, more informed decisions.

26. GAAP standards are all about principles - there are no assumptions and no constraints included in them:

    a. No, GAAP standards consist of principles, assumptions, and constraints;

    b. GAAP standards only include constraints;

    c. GAAP standards only include assumptions;

27. OCBOA is completely accepted as a GAAP alternative:

    a. It is not illegal, but not well-regarded either;

    b. It is basically the same;

    c. No, you should never use OCBOA in any way.

28. Although simpler, OCBOA standards are more extensive than GAAP ones:

    a. Yes, there are 20,000 pages of OCBOA and only 2000 of GAAP;

    b. OCBOA standards are actually more complicated;

    c. No, GAAP standards are far more extensive and regulated than OCBOA - and this is why they are to be used.

29. All the countries in the world have some sort of GAAP system in place and they follow it:

    a. Yes, for instance, countries in EU use EU GAAP;

    b. No, only about 70% of the countries use GAAP;

    c. No, GAAP is used only in the US and a couple other countries, each with their own version of standards.

30. GAAP and IFRS can be used simultaneously with no influence on the final result:

    a. Yes, they are complementary;

b. Yes, they are one and the same, but with different names due to different institutions releasing and monitoring them;

c. No, they are different and should not be used at the same time on the same financial statement.

31. The going concern principle is:

    a. A generally accepted accounting principle in which the financial statement assumes that the business will continue its operations;

    b. An accounting principle (or assumption) that says businesses should assume to be functional only for one more year;

    c. An accounting constraint in which companies that have to go abroad are allowed to use IFRS on US territory.

32. As a business owner, you can use the same bank account and the same accounting paperwork for your individual needs and your personal needs:

    a. Yes, you are the same entity;

    b. No, you need different accounts and different accounting made on your individual account and on your business account;

    c. It doesn't matter, you can do whatever is best for you.

33. The generally accepted accounting principle according to which businesses are assumed to go on is called "the materiality principle":

    a. Yes;

    b. No;

    c. No, it is called "the matching principle".

34. GAAP allows you to use immeasurable qualities (such as the dedication of your development team) as a unit in your financial statements:

    a. Yes, you measure it in money;

    b. Yes, you measure it in percentages;

    c. No, GAAP does not allow you to use such qualities as a unit in financial statements.

35. GAAP is mostly about cash-based accounting:

    a. It is ONLY about cash-based accounting;

    b. No, most of the basic GAAP rules are about accrual accounting, but cash-based accounting rules exist and should be followed as well;

    c. Cash-based accounting is illegal.

36. All assets should be recorded on balance sheets and financial statements at their current market value:

    a. Yes, always;

    b. Yes, but only when the market value has increased the historical cost by 50% or more;

    c. No, the historical cost should be used.

37. Revenue can be recognized at any time, as you deem suitable for the production of a beneficial financial statement:

    a. Yes, the purpose of a financial statement is to make your company look good.

    b. No, revenue can be recognized solely when the cash reaches your company;

    c. No, revenue should be recognized according to the accounting method you have chosen (accrual, cash-based, and so on).

38. The matching principle refers to matching the accounting standards your company uses to the accounting standards your partners use.

    a. Yes;

    b. No, it's about the recognition of expenses;

    c. Yes, but only when the two companies are in different countries.

39. The materiality principle allows companies to not enter certain transactions on their statements, and these transactions can be as large or as small as it is deemed appropriate by the company :

    a. Yes;

    b. No, this is 100% forbidden;

    c. Yes, but only when those transactions are very small (immaterial).

40. When using non-GAAP measures, the management should not be involved in the disclosure preparations:

    a. Yes;

    b. No, only auditing companies should be involved at all times;

    c. It is a matter of what the company decides and the specificities of the situation.

41. You can switch from one accounting method to another from one year to another, as you deem more suitable for your company;

    a. Yes, financial statements are meant to help businesses;

    b. No, but you can switch them when needed as long as you don't abuse this;

    c. No, this should never be done in the lifetime of your business.

42. You have to be consistent in your reporting methods no matter what happens, throughout the entire duration of your business:

    a. Yes;

    b. No;

    c. You can switch to a different reporting method as long as this is disclosed and as long as you remain consistent in your choice.

43. When in doubt, the potential transaction with the most beneficial value to the company should be written on the statements of the company:

    a. Yes, financial statements have to make the company look good;

    b. It depends on what you need;

    c. No, this goes against the conservatism principle.

44. According to IFRS, if the cost of including a piece of information in your financial statements is larger than the benefits of including it, you can omit doing this:

    a. Yes, but this happens very rarely, actually;

    b. Yes, and this happens very often.

    c. No, this is 100% forbidden.

45. OCBOA is not a permitted set of accounting standards and it functions outside of the current legislation of the US:

    a. Yes, OCBOA is illegal;

    b. No, OCBOA can be used, but it is not recommended;

    c. OCBOA is drawn by private investors, but it is not to be used in financial statements under any circumstances.

46. IFRS standards are rule-based, very strict, and enforced in only a handful of countries

    a. No, they are principle-based;

    b. Yes, but there are gateways;

    c. Yes.

47. The European Union developed the IFRS standards:

    a. Yes;

    b. No, they were among the last adopters;

    c. No, they were the second adopters.

48. Australia uses a GAAP accounting system:

    a. Yes, similarly to the US;

    b. No, they have switched to a national version of IFRS;

    c. They use neither GAAP, nor IFRS.

49. India was one of the early adopters of international financial reporting standards:

    a. Yes, they invented it;

    b. No, they are among the last full adopters;

    c. They are still phasing it in.

50. LIFO inventory measures are forbidden under IFRS accounting standards.

    a. Only under certain circumstances;

    b. No, they are allowed;

    c. Yes, they are forbidden.

Correct Answers:

1. b. The US GAAP are rule-based.

2. The US GAAP are actual rules.

3. They are very different in nature.

4. Only domestic companies have to abide by GAAP, SEC-registered foreign companies don't have to.

5. No, all domestic companies should follow GAAP.

6. There are 5 constraints, 4 principles, and 4 assumptions.

7. b. No, FASB is a national (US) organization.

8. b. No. About 120 countries use IFRS.

9. b. No, US companies should use GAAP.

10. Non-GAAP measures can be used, but they have to be clearly disclosed.

11. b. While not always the case, non-GAAP measures can be quite misleading.

12. b. GAAP measures are rule-based, but their use has caused major scandals in the past.

13. Zimbabwe is a good example in how IFRS can be unsuitable in some circumstances, such as hyperinflationary economies.

14. The Enron scandal is one of the most commonly-referred scandals connected to bad use of GAAP standards.

15. Yes, but they have to be justified and disclosed. Furthermore, they still have to be connected to GAAP standards.

16. b. GAAP standards do not function as legislation, but as rules to help accountants and companies abide to the current legislation.

17. GAAP should be used in the US.

18. GAAP does not lead to companies paying more in taxes.

19. No, GAAP standards are monitored by FASB, which is a private board.

20. b. Although FASB is non-governmental, they do communicate with dedicated governmental agencies when it comes to the release and monitoring of accounting standards.

21. Most of the time, the release of new accounting rules and standards is connected to various governmental and non-governmental organizations (including lobbyists).

22. b. SMBs sometimes have to rely on non-GAAP measures.

23. b. Only domestic companies in the US have to use GAAP.

24. b. GAAP rules have to exist and be used. While the US might move to an IFRS-based accounting standard, for now, the GAAP rules should be used to ensure the comparability and transparency of financial statements released by companies.

25. GAAP measures are meant to help users of financial statements - such as investors and creditors.

26. What is known as "GAAP" consists of 5 constraints, 4 principles, and 4 assumptions.

27. OCBOA can be misleading, especially as disclosure standards are not as clear as in GAAP.

28. OCBOA standards are much more simplified.

29. At the moment, most countries use IFRS or other national-based accounting standards. GAAP is used in the USA and a couple other countries.

30. They are different standardization systems, and thus, they should not be used simultaneously.

31. The going concern principle is the GAAP rule in which financial statement assume that the business will continue its operations;

32. Under the business entity principle, you are required to run different accounting paperwork for your personal and business accounts.

33. No, it is called the "going concern principle".

34. No, and this is one of the main criticisms brought to GAAP. IFRS, on the other hand, does allow these kinds of qualities to be included in financial statements.

35. b. Most of the basic rules of GAAP refer to accrual accounting, but there are rules set in place for cash-based and other types of accounting as well.

36. Under GAAP, the historical cost should be used.

37. Revenue can be recognized at different times, according to the type of accounting you have adopted. For instance, in accrual accounting, revenue is to be recognized when your buyer receives the goods/services.

38. b. The matching principle is the other side of the coin of the revenue recognition principle, and it refers to expenses.

39. Yes, certain transactions can be left off of balance sheets and statements, but only as long as they are very small (and how

small is deemed immaterial depends on the company, its revenue, the nature of those transactions, and so on).

40. It depends. In most situations the management has to be involved. There are cases however when the disclosure committee is a sub-branch of the board. There are also cases when auditors are involved as well.

41. b. You can switch from one accounting method to another - but your change has to be consistent (so you cannot change back or to another accounting method in the next accounting period).

42. You don't have to stick to the same accounting method throughout the life of your business. When doing a switch, however, this has to be fully disclosed. Even more so, it has to be a change that leads to consistency.

43. According to the conservatism principle, the least favorable outcome should be used for the purpose of reporting.

44. Yes, GAAP allows this - but it happens very rarely that companies meet the criteria to deem a piece of information too expensive to acquire and report.

45. OCBOA can be used, but it functions outside of GAAP (as a non-GAAP), and it might mislead readers of financial statements if not properly disclosed.

46. IFRS are principle-based, as opposed to GAAP.

47. Yes, the EU was the first to develop IFRS, out of the need they had to connect different accounting standards present across countries of the European Union.

48. Australia used a GAAP system, but they have switched to an Australian version of IFRS (called A-IFRS).

49. As of 2016, India is phasing in the IFRS system.

50. This is one of the major differences between GAAP and IFRS: LIFO inventory can be used in the case of the former, but not in the case of the latter.

Conclusion

For outside viewers, the world of accounting is all about addition and subtraction, numbers, and endless spreadsheets.

For those truly passionate about this field of expertise, accounting is about much more than numbers. Sure, arithmetic plays a pretty important role in everything - but at the end of the day, accounting is about growing businesses, about law, about being part of a national system of rules and regulations (not just from an economic point of view, but from a social point of view as well).

Businesses happen on multiple fronts.

There is the front stage, where salespeople in shiny suits sell products and services that have been beautifully dressed by the marketing pros.

And then there is the backstage - the spreadsheets and statements where it all happens. The place where accountants, auditors, managers, and assistants analyze, dissect, and find the best solutions for the best growth.

As an accountant, you are part of a machine that is bigger than you - but you are not a simple cog without which the machinery would keep on going. You are the very oil running the machine.

Without great accounting, even the largest companies can easily fall - and the Enron example we have referred to throughout this book is a very comprehensive portrayal of how things can go wrong when accountants work on the dark side of accounting regulations.

As an accountant, you hold great power and great responsibility as well. You have the power to put your company in the best of lights, but also the responsibility to do this correctly and in the spirit of full transparency to all parties involved. Your responsibility lies with your employer, sure, but beyond that, it lies with the entire financial community. It lies with the entire economy of your country. It lies with society at large who expect that every business be a functional and prosperous member of it.

This book is, hopefully, an incursion into the magnificent and intricate world of accounting, into the subtleties that make it fascinating and into the brick and mortar that make it clear and understandable beyond the numbers.

As I mentioned in the beginning, this book's purpose is to offer you a basic understanding of how accounting works behind the curtains and the spreadsheets. The intricacies of a world that's frequently minimized into cells, columns, and formulae are, indeed, interesting - both to those of you who have just started out on this path and to those of you simply curious of how the micro-machinery of accounting functions in the context of a larger machine called *the economy*.

As you have noticed, our focus lies mostly with generally accepted accounting principles, as the main rules accountants in the United States have to use. We have, however, dipped our toes into non-GAAP and IFRS measures too - enough to show you how the world beyond GAAP works, and what the advantages and disadvantages of other systems of standards used both inside and outside of the US.

We hope the information provided in this book has proved useful to novices and the merely curious. And we hope you will continue to investigate the complexities of accounting standards from hereon as well.

The world needs excellent accountants. Research, work hard, and dedicate yourself to being more than companies want you to be. Be the professional the world needs you to be!

Made in the USA
Columbia, SC
05 June 2019